Die Before They Do

From selling drugs to lunch with Jim Carrey.
Stories of struggle, near death experiences,
and creating a life with meaning.

Robb Gilbear

This is a work of non-fiction. However, certain names, identifying details, or characteristics of individuals have been changed.

GROWTH HABIT

Growth Habit

ISBN 978-1-7779390-0-7

Cover design by Nick Kopa

Author photos by Chris "Kotsy" Kotsopoulos

First edition 2021

growthhabit.org

Keep doing bold shit + work with impact

For the creative, curious, entrepreneurial, rebellious, and empathetic souls who know they're meant to do more.

Contents

1. Selling Drugs 8

2. Struggles and Misadventures 16

3. Dirty Cash 20

4. Grandfather Clock 25

5. Cube Van 32

6. Acid Trip 38

7. All That Money 44

8. Selling Records 48

9. Whoops 55

10. Cliff Jumping 61

11. Vancouver Local Rate 66

12. $50 Bonus 70

13. Daft Punk 74

14. Watch Me Do Homework 79

15. Without A Paddle 82

16. 12 Inch Therapy 88

17. Shambhala 95

18. KK Papa 102

19. The Seizure 107

20. Affording It 113

21. Get Out of Here 117

22. Suicide 122

23. Going Viral 126

24. Begging and Pleading 129

25. Halloween Tuxedo 132

26. Celebrate Mondays 137

27. No You Didn't 141

28. Eulogy 151

29. You Can't Do That 158

30. Starts With A Kiss 162

31. Second Date 165

32. How Things Feel 172

33. Nuberto 176

34. Dancing in Seoul 182

35. People Mistakes 186

36. We'll Break You 196

37. Fake Dates 202

38. Rich People Are Assholes 205

39. Dancing In Paris 209

40. Five Years From Now 215

41. Habit Tracking 219

42. Pop Fly 223

43. Halfway There 226

44. You Don't Need Us 234

45. December 10th 238

46. Take a Chance on Me 242

47. Loose Goals 245

48. Die Before They Do 250

Acknowledgements 253

About the Author 259

1

Selling Drugs

"I know someone in Toronto who'll sell us 1000 hits for $1000. A buck a piece."

That was James. He was always looking for a way to make some money.

Back in the 1990s, the going rate for LSD was $5 a hit. If you were lucky, you could get five hits of acid for $20 when someone was trying to move their inventory.

"We could go in on buying a thousand hits together and split it. Robb, do you think you could handle selling 200 hits?"

My mind quickly did the math: I could turn $200 into $1000. That was a lot of money to 17-year-old me.

It was 1995, Kurt Cobain had died the year before and Tupac was still alive. Most people didn't have cell phones and if you were one of the few people regularly using the Internet, you were likely using Netscape to browse online.

While my mom and dad struggled with their marriage due to my dad's extended absences from being in the army, I found an escape from the monotony and boredom of small town life in the creative and welcoming atmosphere of raves. I was obsessed with collecting music and loved how dancing brought people together. Even though I was already DJing at small one-off events in my area, I dreamed of playing big events in the city. I had bleached blond hair parted down the middle, my wardrobe consisted of baggy jeans and striped T-shirts, and now I was contemplating selling acid.

The opportunity to make quick cash was enticing, but I hadn't sold drugs on this scale before. While I was no stranger to picking up extra stuff for friends when making my own purchases, this was new territory to me. The only way I could move that much acid was if I started selling to strangers. Saying yes meant I was going to be a drug dealer. Undeniably.

A week later, midday on a Wednesday, James and I hopped into his girlfriend Jessica's Volkswagen to go make the purchase. Jessica had big, black wavy hair, rosy cheeks, and a round face. She wore baggy plaid shirts and had an awesome taste in music that ranged from underground house music to Prodigy and Ministry.

The three of us hung out often. Only this time, instead of his usual animated self, James was oddly quiet. The nervous energy in the car was a contrast to our Saturday night drives to parties in the city. On those trips, drum & bass would be blasting from the speakers while more people than there were seat belts would be packed into Jessica's little hatchback. This was a different kind of outing. We were meeting with a big-time city drug dealer. My mind raced as I noticed small details in Jessica's car I'd never seen before. Was the interior ceiling always grey? When did those burn marks get up there?

We met the dealer at the edge of a run-down mall parking lot in a part of Toronto I wasn't familiar with. As we pulled into the nearly empty lot, I felt like we were moving in slow motion. The pavement was beat up and uneven and the metal posts holding the mall signs were rusted. The dealer was confidently standing in the open at the edge of the parking lot, wearing black jeans, a black leather jacket, and black sunglasses. His face showed no emotion as he restrained his hungry-looking Rottweiler on a short leash.

I could hear my heartbeat as James stepped out of the car. Neither Jessica nor I said a word as we watched him walk slowly toward the man and his dog.

I held my breath as they made the transaction. James handed him an envelope. The man in black looked at the money inside before putting it in his front pocket. He then pulled an envelope of his own out of his back pocket and handed it to James. They both nodded before James turned around. The exchange was over in less than two minutes.

I don't know that I'd ever seen Jessica follow the rules of the road so closely as she did on that drive home. Full stops, no running of yellow lights, signalling every lane change, and taking the speed limit at face value. You'd have thought she was doing her driving test with a police cruiser behind her. No one said a word. I tried to calm my nerves and distract myself by thinking about what music equipment I'd buy with the money I'd make.

The first 30 hits were easy to sell. They were gone Wednesday night thanks to friends who were waiting for them. It was getting rid of the other 170 that was going to require work, even though, with over 1,800 students and no shortage of stoners, my high school was the perfect marketplace.

I hesitated in the doorway before walking into the school building that Thursday morning. The students and teachers milling around me didn't know what I had in my backpack, but I did. What if I got caught? What would my parents say? Would I go to jail? Someone in a rush bumped into me as they ran past. It knocked me out of that spiral of thoughts.

Feeling reluctant to blow my cover, I was slow to tell people what I had for sale. By last period, I built up the courage to share with a couple of classmates. They each bought one after class. Only 168 more to go.

Friends helped me get rid of 15 more that Thursday night but I quickly realized that it wasn't a sustainable business model when my mom asked why so many people were coming by the house. I really needed to off-load these somewhere else.

My classmates/clients from the previous day found me standing in front of the school on Friday morning before the bell rang. They had done the hits last night, loved them, and were back for more.

They also helped spread the word by telling their friends. By Friday afternoon, people were seeking me out. I set up shop in the back of the cafeteria with a backpack on each side of me on the table to provide some cover for the transactions. The constant flow of customers made time pass quickly.

As I packed up Friday afternoon, my pockets were overflowing with cash, including a suspicious amount of $5 bills. I didn't know the exact number of hits I had left as I hadn't had time to pause and count. I did know, however, that I had moved more than 100 since I left the house that morning because I had ripped through the ones in my backpack's front pouch and had to go to the second batch I had stashed in the back of my Grade 11 math textbook.

I ran into James in the hall on my way to the buses behind the school. The big grin on his face and bounce in his step told me that he'd had an equally successful day. He had sold several dozen hits to a single person. She said she was going to come back for more next week, too. He was beaming.

My happiness for him quickly turned to jealousy when I found out who the buyer was. Samantha was an old co-worker of mine. We had worked together at McDonald's and we were friends. We'd hung out outside of work and I'd been to her house. James barely knew her.

That should've been me, I thought. That should've been my sale. Fuck.

Trying not to stew on the lost opportunity, I focused on getting rid of a few more hits of acid that weekend. I came back to school on Monday with less than 20 to go. This was easy.

It was lunchtime when I saw Jessica barrelling towards me. Her cheeks were flushed and redder than usual and her eyes were full of concern. Something was wrong.

"Samantha got busted for selling acid. She told the cops that she got them from James. They raided his locker and found his stash. James was arrested."

I was out of the building and off school property within minutes. My body shook as the questions cycled through my head. Did Samantha know that I was selling? Would James give me up to ease the pressure on him? Would someone else get caught and give me up? The "That should've been me" that I was telling myself earlier was now "That *could've* been me."

In the following days and weeks, I was frantic. I barely slept and missed more school than usual.

The few times I did make it to class, I couldn't concentrate, expecting a cop to walk in looking for me at any moment.

It took over a month, but eventually I realized that nothing was going to happen. I could be on school grounds without feeling tense. I knew I was in the clear.

Although I'd got a taste of making real money that far exceeded my part-time job hourly pay for flipping burgers, I realized I'd have to find another outlet for my entrepreneurial aspirations.

I knew I wanted independence and a way out of small town life, but this wasn't the ticket. I wanted to do something I felt passionate about. Something that helped others.

And while the close call was enough to put my drug dealing days to an end, I'd need another scare to stop taking LSD recreationally.

2

Struggles and Misadventures

Hey there, I'm Robb Gilbear. What you're holding in your hands is a collection of stories that tell my journey through entrepreneurship, self-doubt, massive career changes, struggles with alcohol, near death experiences, an obsession with music, finding love, and being a parent, all while searching for bigger meaning and purpose.

You could easily say that me writing a book was unlikely. I dropped out of high school and never went to college or university. Instead, I started my first business as a teenager.

I also had a late start at reading books just for fun. It wasn't until my Grade 11 English teacher, Miss Lewis, gave me a copy of George Orwell's *1984*, pleading with me because she didn't want me to fail her class, that I finally got hooked.

"Just read the first two chapters," she said. "If you read the first two chapters and really hate it, then let me know, and we'll figure out another assignment for you so you can pass this class."

She was certain I was going to like it, and she was right. I loved the book and devoured it in a matter of days. The story resonated with my rebellious ways and belief in the need for counterculture instead of blindly following what everyone else was doing.

Fanning the flame of my newfound interest in reading, my Grade 11 girlfriend gave me a copy of Douglas Coupland's *Shampoo Planet*. That one didn't last nearly as long as I read most of the novel in one sitting during an all-nighter at Cheers Donuts in Tottenham, Ontario.

It was a book about discovery and identity. It's the story of a young man who wants to find his purpose and make it in the world of business. The book plays with the idea of escaping from a regular life to do something enlightening and fulfilling. Part philosophical, it's also provocative and hilarious.

These days, I often have two or three different books on the go at a time. While I didn't pursue any formal post-secondary education beyond one-off courses that interested me, I never stopped learning. The growth I've been able to experience thanks to my love for reading has been invaluable. I'm immensely grateful for it.

The spark for me to write a book came from an improbable place: social media. I was writing regularly to share my thoughts and ideas online. On LinkedIn, I found a community supportive of my reflections on business and my personal experiences.

Whenever I openly shared tales of my personal struggles and misadventures, I'd get messages from people thanking me. Telling me they felt seen, understood, and that they could relate. That it gave them hope and helped them realize that maybe there is another way.

Some of those stories are wild and entertaining. Some are more profound. I've faced divorce while simultaneously walking away from a 20-year career as a DJ and music producer. It drove me into a pit of depression and challenged the assumptions of who I was. I've had to completely reinvent myself on more than one occasion and I'm a firm believer that your past does not need to equal your future.

With this book, I didn't set out to write a story about the journey of my life. I never intended my first book to be about me.

My hope is that by sharing my story, you'll see that regardless of where you come from, you can be the intentional creator of your life.

3

Dirty Cash

A deep sense of empathy for others and a fond love of music with a strong beat—these are the two things that I'm most grateful for that my mom instilled in me. The appreciation for music started young. When I was a toddler, she'd blast Lipps Inc's "Funkytown" and Babe Ruth's "The Mexican" on our big, brown all-in-one stereo system.

By Grade 4, I had rigged my own little stereo in my bedroom with begged and borrowed parts. I made regular trips to the local department store for the latest 45 singles and cassette tapes using money from my after-school paper route.

My babysitter Todd, and his beautiful wood panel Radio Shack mixer, made me eclectic mix tapes that flowed from Beastie Boys to Wham. I was fascinated by his ability to blend one song into the other with that funky-looking box. My mom even convinced him to DJ my backyard birthday party when I was 10.

I'd get my first crack at DJing the following year in England when my dad was posted overseas for work and we landed at an army base an hour and a half northwest of London. In between trying to understand mandatory school uniforms and being harassed for my "funny accent," I continued to obsessively collect music.

The sounds I was being exposed to in England were vastly different than in Canada as house music was exploding in the U.K. in the late '80s. During the year and a half we were there, I was introduced to the likes of Rebel MC, A Guy Called Gerald, S'Express, and 808 State. It was music from the future, but with the familiar disco rhythms that reminded me of the records my mom played when I was a kid. It was a dream to dance to, and dancing became my refuge.

At home, isolated and homesick, my mom was struggling with depression. New to the neighbourhood and with a weird accent and clothes that didn't match what the locals wore, I was being bullied. And while we attended different schools, my brother and I were both having run-ins with teachers and getting into trouble.

My anger, my loneliness, and all my feelings of uncertainty dimmed when I closed my eyes and moved to music. I spent every night I could at the local youth club—a windowless concrete building that was painted entirely black on the inside, and was full of speakers and flashing lights. Sure, I socialized, but I was there to hear the music and move my body and dance. It was there, on an army base off the M40 motorway in the English Midlands, that I got my first taste of mixing two records together.

The club's regular DJ knew me well. I was consistently the first one on the dance floor and often asked questions about the tracks he was playing. One night, as I was asking for the name of a song he played, he pulled me into the booth.

"You love the music so much, why don't you have a go?" he asked.

He handed me the headphones and my hands moved cautiously on the faders as I brought in the horns and breaks from Stevie V's "Dirty Cash." I watched the smiling crowd dance to the music I was playing and thought: This is something I could see myself doing.

When we landed back in Canada 18 months later, settling in at an army base 90 minutes north of Toronto, I sought out the local teen club with gusto and newfound confidence. Hip hop was all the rage and our town's teen club acted as the weekly gathering spot for big Saturday night dances that attracted kids from all the neighbouring towns. The dance floor became the battleground for weekly dance-offs that often pitted the different towns against one another. I was no stranger to the centre of those dance circles, and the tension escalated to physical fights on more than one occasion.

Thanks to an endorsement by my mom's best friend, I got a part-time job at the local McDonald's to keep me out of trouble. I was happy as it gave me a steady stream of money to buy music with. It wasn't long until I had hundreds of CDs and cassettes in my collection. I continued going to the dances, and when I wasn't on the dance floor, I was hanging out by the DJ booth.

The transient way of military life meant that teen club DJs often came and went in a short period of time. I seemed to play the same role regardless of the DJ: I brought in my music to supplement theirs and advised on the genres they were less knowledgeable about. In return, I got to mix in the odd song while receiving lessons on track selection and programming sets.

Finally, in the summer of 1994, when the next DJ moved away, I was offered the gig. I was 16 years old and had landed my first DJ residency.

If I only knew where this love of music was going to lead me.

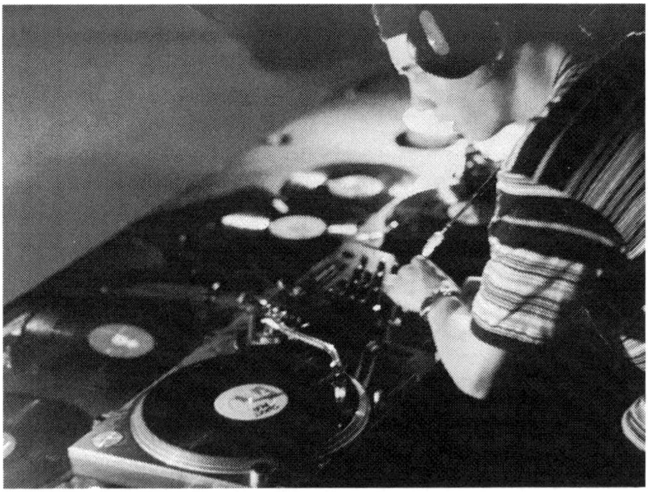

DJing in Alliston in the mid '90s

Robb Gilbear

4

Grandfather Clock

When you grow up in a military family, either you're moving around because your parents have been posted, or your friends are. I can't recall one summer growing up where a close friend of mine wasn't moving away or I wasn't saying teary-eyed goodbyes to all of my friends because we were the ones being transferred.

The summer between Grade 8 and 9 was a doozy. The high school on the army base where we lived was closing down. For English-speaking kids, that meant a 15-minute drive to a new school. For French-speaking kids like me, the closest French high school was going to be over an hour away.

I was raised bilingual but often say that French is my mother tongue as I revert to French whenever I'm counting or swearing. I learned English from my mom and French from my dad. My dad was born and raised in rural Québec. He only learned English in his late teens when he had to take mandatory English classes after enlisting in the army. We lived in Québec for six years from when I was two to eight years old. That's where I started school and that's where my younger brother was born. Even when we moved to Base Borden in Ontario, I stayed in French schools that were full of Québecois teachers.

Since the local high school was now closing down and the French school was over an hour away, French-speaking families with high school-aged kids were given a moving priority that year. We stayed put but instead of *some* of my friends being transferred that summer, most of them were.

I started hanging out with new kids. Running in new circles and trying to find my place. In one group, stealing from the local department store was what they did for kicks. It wasn't something I could push myself to do. Another crew thought it would be "funny" to brand me with a burning hot lighter after they had gotten me drunk.

One of the new friends I started hanging out with was Rick. He was an instigator but he was hilarious, polite around parents, and had a knack for finding a good time. He let me know about a hangout spot where friends of his were having fun. Someone's parents had gone on vacation for a couple of weeks and left their teenage daughter to stay with friends. What those parents didn't know was that their daughter, Lucie, had made a copy of the house key and was letting friends in while they were out of town. Dozens of kids were coming and going from the house every day.

I tried playing it cool when we showed up. I had never been anywhere like this. There were people getting drunk in the living room, kids smoking weed in the backyard, and teenagers having sex upstairs. It was like a scene out of a movie.

We spent several days in a row at Lucie's house and then one morning, Rick came by my house and asked if I had heard the news. The neighbours had called the cops. They cleared everyone out.

"Want to go check it out?" Rick asked.

I was curious and what the hell were we going to do anyway? We made our way to Lucie's house and sure enough, the door was locked. We rang the doorbell. There was no one there.

As we walked around the house, Rick noticed a back window was open.

"Should we go in?" he asked.

We both knew he was going in regardless of what I said. He opened the window all the way, pulled himself up onto the windowsill, and climbed through. He unlocked the back door for me to join him.

It was eerie being inside the house now. We were never supposed to be there before, but someone who lived there had let us in previously. Now we were clearly doing something illegal. The house smelled like cigarettes, teen body odour, and stale beer. Dirty dishes and empty bottles of booze were everywhere downstairs, while clothes and empty condom wrappers littered the floors upstairs.

We weren't in the house long before we started making things worse. Rick knocked over a vase and said "Oops," but it wasn't an accident. It escalated into a game of one-upping each other. After the vase, I smashed some plates. After the plates were broken, he knocked over the grandfather clock.

We were in and out of the house in less than 30 minutes. The cure for our boredom that day was senselessly causing hundreds of dollars worth of damage to someone else's belongings.

After being notified by the police of what their daughter had been up to, Lucie's parents cut their trip short and came home early. To their surprise, their house was in much worse shape than they had anticipated thanks to our reckless behaviour. Hoping to find the culprits of the additional damage, the cops rounded up several of us who had been at the house the previous week.

Before I knew it, I was sitting in a small police interrogation room with my parents while a military police officer began asking me questions. The officer let us know that several others were in the rooms down the hall. Still, I refused to talk. So did everyone else. I tried calling the number given to us by the police for free legal aid services to get advice from a lawyer but I couldn't get through.

Several hours passed and the cops were getting frustrated. No one was talking.

My mom, refusing to believe that I could've done anything wrong, was argumentative with the police.

My father, who I had a strained relationship with, was quiet. He was embarrassed to be there.

Dad was a dedicated military man who was often out of town, and sometimes out of the country. Since he wasn't around the house much, I didn't really know him and I definitely felt like he didn't know me. He had a temper, and when I reached my teens and he started being around more, we really clashed.

Needing a break, my father left the room to walk off the stress. He came back a little while later to try to encourage me to talk.

"The cops say that all legal aid will advise you to do is to not say anything, but not cooperating would look bad in the eyes of the judge," he said to me.

Moments later, a different police officer entered the room with a beat-up blue folder full of papers. He dramatically dropped it on the desk.

"Rick says you're the one who did the grandfather clock," he said.

"That's bullshit!" I cried out. "He broke the clock, I smashed the plates."

As quickly as that, I went from not saying a word for hours to falling for one of the oldest police tricks in the book.

Once the police had my full confession, it was easy for them to get Rick to talk.

Both Rick and I were charged with unlawful entry, theft under $5000, and mischief causing damage under $5000. We were fingerprinted and told we'd have to appear in court before being sent home.

A few months later, wearing a dress shirt that was three sizes too big tucked into pants that were equally oversized, I stood in front of a judge.

"The only thing holding me back from locking you up is not wanting to put you away over the holidays on your first offence," the judge said as he read out his verdict.

I was fined $450 dollars to repay damages. I was also given 50 hours of community service, and put on probation for 12 months. One of the terms of the probation was that Rick and I couldn't hang out with each other any more. I'd have to find new friends and a new community to keep me company. Hopefully one that didn't lead to so much trouble.

5

Cube Van

Once someone brought me to my first rave in Grade 9, I was hooked. The DJs played underground electronic music on massive sound systems that made you feel the bass throughout your body. Held in secret locations that weren't revealed until the day of the event, the raves were all about music and dancing. No one was drinking and there wasn't a hint of the aggression I'd encountered at the teen club dances.

In the '90s rave scene, I found a creative and open-minded community. One that didn't care about what part of town you were from or what clothes you wore. It was an accepting place where your ethnicity, gender, sexual orientation, or expression didn't matter. It was normal to find hippies, drag queens, and business executives all dancing side by side. No one cared.

It felt like a utopia compared to the dismal small town life full of fighting and petty crime that I was used to. Peace, Love, Unity, Respect (P.L.U.R.) was the credo printed on the back of many rave party flyers. Raving gave me a family of friends who cared about others and loved to dance. It gave me hope.

Since I lived in Borden, an hour and a half outside of Toronto, the trek to the parties in the city was half the adventure. Seeing an opportunity, entrepreneurial teens in my area arranged shuttle buses to the events.

If you were a party goer, you'd get a secure ride there and back, entry to the party, and skip the big lineup upon arrival. This was a real bonus as the queue outside of the parties was often hundreds, if not thousands, of people long.

If you were the one putting on the rave, you got a guaranteed bulk purchase of 50-70 tickets to your event in exchange for giving away one free ticket and letting a group skip the line.

That free ticket went to the person arranging the bus. Not only did that person get into the event for free, but they were also swimming in status points. When you're the one organizing things, everyone knows your name and everyone wants to hang out with you.

Swirling in the energy of anticipation, the bus rides down to Toronto were a blast. They were the best pre-party, and the perfect place to make new friends, as well as catch up with old ones. We swapped mix tapes of the latest DJ sets while discussing the venue and who we were excited to see.

Given the nature of the crowd, the buses were often hot-boxed with the copious amounts of weed being smoked during the ride. Most of the time, the bus drivers would be cool with it and simply ask us to roll down the windows.

One night, we got an older driver. He wore khaki slacks, white running shoes, and a loose-fitting golf shirt, and had a head of wiry grey hair.

"There's enough reefer on this bus to get the bus driver high!" he shouted as he pulled the bus over on the side of a six-lane highway 20 minutes into the trip. He turned on the sobering interior lights and yelled at us. "If it doesn't stop right now, I'm calling the police." That put an end to weed on that particular trip.

One Saturday—September 9, 1995, to be exact—I missed the shuttle due to work and made my own way to an event downtown. I know the precise day because I still have the newspaper clipping.

I met up with friends when I got to the party and we danced the night away. As the event was winding down the next morning, I handed the shuttle organizer $5 to catch a ride home with the others on the bus.

It wasn't until we got to the parking lot that I discovered there wasn't a bus. Instead, there was a cube van with mattresses on the floor. I paused as the other 33 teens started piling in.

"Don't worry, it's comfier than it looks. It was fine on the way down," said a friend as she got in ahead of me.

Since I had paused before climbing in, I was one of the last ones onboard. I ended up in the left corner near the back door and on the edge of one of the mattresses.

After adjusting to the bumpiness due to the poor shocks, I settled in. I was feeling tired and grateful to have a ride instead of having to deal with spending hours on public transit. A few people cuddled up and some passed out. It was quiet.

We were halfway home when I heard the scream. That familiar roller coaster feeling in my belly followed.

The van flew off the road, became airborne, and landed in a ditch that was a 15-foot drop from the highway. We hit the ground with a violent thud. Everyone went flying. There were people screaming, and more than one person was bleeding. It was chaos and confusion as we all tried to untangle ourselves.

There were so many injuries that the police sent an ambulance *bus*. Imagine a big full-length bus that's been converted and equipped to be an ambulance that can tend to numerous people at once.

The list of injuries reported in the newspaper included broken ankles, a broken jaw, and a broken back. I was one of the lucky ones, only suffering from cuts and a twisted ankle.

"One thing saved you all from a 50% fatality rate," said the senior police officer on the scene.

"If the ground wasn't wet, that van would've rolled instead of sinking into the grass, and half of you would've been dead."

A few days of rain had saved our asses.

I'd never been one to follow the crowd. Doing so this time around had almost killed me.

6

Acid Trip

The right thing to do would've been to tell them that I was high on LSD.

The problem with being so high on acid that you feel you need to go to the emergency room is that there's no guarantee that you'll do the sensible thing once you get there.

Friends and I had organized an after-hours event in Alliston, the town where my high school was located, 20 minutes from Borden. We'd arranged a deal with a local bar to use their space after they were done for the night. We set up our gear and started our party at 2 a.m. with DJs scheduled to play until 8 in the morning.

I DJed in one of the opening time slots and was tired. I had worked earlier in the day and spent the evening selling tickets and getting my music ready. After my set, I ate one sole hit of acid. I wasn't looking to get super high. I just wanted it to stay awake and carry me through the night.

Usually—for me anyway—an acid trip feels wonderful and euphoric. Colours are more vibrant, words have deeper meaning, and you see the interconnectivity of everything around you.

This, however, quickly turned into a very different kind of trip. Forty-five minutes after I took the hit of acid, my heart was pounding so hard that it was difficult to dance. I took a seat. My heart felt like it might punch through my chest even though I was sitting still. I focused on my breath and tried to get my pulse down. It wasn't working. It was only getting worse. My heart rate was so high that I was having difficulty breathing.

Of course I'd heard the horror stories about people having a bad trip on acid. Things like people jumping off a roof because they thought they could fly, or falling into a paranoid psychosis, but that had never been my experience.

I'd been doing LSD casually for a few years. It was a fun and cheap escape. I enjoyed how it opened up my perception of the world and got me to see things differently. Up to that point, the worst thing that had come out of my acid trips was the bad poetry I'd written. There's probably still some of that drivel in boxes in my parents' basement.

As I struggled to stay calm while dancers moved around me, I started asking around, looking for someone who was sober and had a car. We were only a few minutes away from the local hospital but I couldn't make the walk. The girl I was seeing got a friend of hers to drive us both there. I knew I needed help.

When we got there, the emergency room was quiet and there was no one else waiting, but it was still intense. The bright fluorescent lights and white walls were blinding. Two nurses got me into a bed and hooked me up to a heart monitor—160 beats per minute was my resting heart rate.

To give you some context, a normal resting heart rate is between 60 to 100 beats per minute. One hundred and sixty beats per minute is the upper limit of what my heart rate should've been if I was sprinting full out. But I wasn't sprinting. I was laying still in a hospital bed.

Had I been in a bigger city, the jig would've been up. But this was a small town hospital that wasn't used to teenagers coming in the middle of the night high on drugs.

The nurses and doctors ran tests and asked so many questions that I felt dizzy. I answered every single one as truthfully as possible. All except for the most important one, which is when they asked if I'd taken any substances.

They inserted an intravenous needle into the back of my left hand and injected me with what the doctor felt confident would slow down my heart rate. It didn't.

Puzzled and looking defeated, the doctor explained that there was something else they could try, a drug that hadn't been actively used in decades. It would take a bit as they needed to go fetch it from a storage room in the hospital's basement. Twenty minutes later a nurse arrived with a stubby brown bottle that had a faded label. She had to dust it off. It looked like a prop from an old movie.

Machines were beeping, lights were flashing, and multiple medical staff were hovering around me while I was tripping balls.

My date for this adventure was sitting dead silent at my bedside with pupils the size of nickels thanks to her own acid trip. She had her black hoodie pulled over her head to minimize her sensory input. I asked her if she was OK. She shook her head.

The doctor prepped the needle and injected me with the solution from the basement while the nurses held their breath. It was almost instantaneous. My heart rate jumped from 158 to 122, then to 88 beats per minute in a matter of seconds. It was as if I'd been hit by a cement truck at full speed. Bam!

The doctor smiled, the nurses' shoulders dropped and they all let out big sighs. The doctor, looking pleased, started walking away.

That didn't last long. Moments later machines around me started going wild, beeping incessantly. My heart rate jumped right back up and hit an all-time high. I saw 192 flash on the screen before it dropped to 186.

"He's rebounding," one nurse yelled. The doctor came running back. I was in immense pain. They stood still. They had no idea what to do.

Over the course of the next couple of hours my heart rate continued to slowly drop: 165, 144, 127, then 110. I could breathe. I wasn't nearly as high anymore, and I wanted to leave.

"We'd really like you to stay. We're concerned for your safety," the doctor said.

"I'm an adult. I checked myself in, and I can check myself out," I said.

I had turned 18 just a few months prior. They argued with me. As I got mad, my heart rate started climbing again. They couldn't keep me against my will so they gave me a pile of paperwork for me to sign.

"This one says you relieve the doctor and all staff on duty of any wrongdoing. This one declares that you can't hold the hospital responsible for anything that happens after you leave. This one states that you can't hold any liability against the province since you're checking yourself out."

I walked out with my date and we made our way back to the party on foot so I could pick up my records. The sun was coming up and I was both physically and mentally exhausted. It would take me weeks to process how scary and surreal the experience was.

That was the last time I did LSD. If I was going to pursue DJing, I realized, I needed to keep my focus on the art of making music and avoid the drugs.

7

All That Money

"Think about what you'll do with all that extra money."

It was June and I was done with high school. By that I mean I was 2.5 credits short of getting my diploma with no plans on going back. I struggled to see the value of much of what was being taught, and the manner in which most subjects were delivered left much to be desired: Sit quietly while you are lectured, read some additional text, memorize and regurgitate—no thank you. I preferred spending my time practising DJing and making money that I could reinvest into music. I saw music as my ticket out.

What had started as a part-time gig flipping burgers five years earlier was now a full-time job as an hourly paid manager. I was well-liked and knew what was expected of me. It was comfortable, routine, and predictable. Music offered me excitement and variety as I was starting to get DJ gigs in the neighbouring cities and towns.

Then my bosses at McDonald's did something I wasn't expecting: They offered me a full-time salaried role, $28,000 a year with benefits. I was 19, still living at home, had few expenses, and I didn't need the benefits. It was a lot of money for me, a significant raise over my current hourly pay.

"Think about what you'll do with all that extra money."

That was one of the senior managers trying to sell me on what my life could be like if I took the role. I could finally buy a car like him and the other managers at the restaurant.

I wasn't thinking of the money, though. I was thinking of what accepting the offer would mean. When I looked at all the salaried managers I worked with, none of them seemed particularly happy. They were making decent money for their needs, but they weren't learning new skills that were moving them forward. They had cars so they could get to work, and they went to work so they could pay for their cars. The shift work meant their personal lives suffered, too. They either struggled to hold down relationships or were already on their second marriage. They seemed stuck. The one I respected the most had confided in me that he had plans to "get out" as he had never intended to work there that long.

The opportunities and paths of small town army base life had always seemed limited: You could join the military like your parents, get a job at the big factory in the nearby town, or get involved in crime. There was nothing wrong with either of the legal options. I just knew they weren't for me. I knew I wanted more. Music had shown me an entire new universe of possibilities.

But if I didn't accept the job, then what? It would've been weird to stay. Once I got into the mindset of possible change, I started re-evaluating everything. In a matter of weeks, I turned down the salaried role, quit McDonald's altogether, broke up with my long-term girlfriend, and moved out of my parents' house. I reset everything.

Knowing the leadership team at work wouldn't be able to process that I was quitting without another job lined up and not wanting to insult them after they'd been so good to me for half a decade, I lied and said I got a job at a factory in Barrie, a small city 30 minutes away where I had been spending more and more of my time. They were sad to see me go but understood the decision.

Even then, though I had no clue what lay ahead or how I'd make money, **I knew I couldn't swim for new horizons without letting go of my current shore.**

8

Selling Records

I met Jay and his brother Trevor at their DJ shop in Barrie, the Beat Boutique. They were older than me, had way more experience as DJs, and were running the staple electronic music night in town at the time. I looked up to Jay like a big brother. When he asked if I wanted to move in with them, I jumped at the chance.

Selling mix tapes and doing DJ gigs around Barrie and in the neighbouring towns was how I was getting by. My hacking around with music ideas had evolved into using a sampler to add creative layers of sounds into my DJ sets. I knew I needed to graduate from being the equivalent of a cover band that only played other people's music if I wanted to break out of being a regional act. I had dreams of performing at bigger events and getting invited to play in different cities. To do that, I needed to start releasing my own original material.

I met Todd through Jay and Trevor. He was a serious gear head obsessed with technology and he built a studio in the back of the Beat Boutique when the store moved to a bigger location. I stood in awe the first time I walked in. There were thousands of dollars worth of drum machines, samplers, effects racks, and computers, all in a cool-looking black room with soundproof walls. It felt like a spaceship control room with all its flashing lights and buttons. It was awesome. Todd and his soon to be studio partner, Sheldon, helped me take my half-baked ideas based on looping samples and turn them into my first original songs.

Now that I was making music, I needed somewhere to put it out. In the late '90s, there were no digital downloads or online streaming. People bought music in physical formats. Favouring its warm sound and tactile interface, DJs still preferred using vinyl records even though CDs were all the rage.

I realized that I didn't know anyone with a record label, or have the faintest idea of how you got music signed to one, so I decided to start my own. Using money I had saved plus a loan from a friend, I launched Laidback Lab Records in the summer of 1998 with a limited run of 300 copies for its first release. I was 20 and had no idea what I was doing.

While others my age went off to college and university, I was trying to figure out the ins and outs of running a record label. Notably, how the hell to sell the boxes of 12-inch records that were now piled up in my bedroom.

Jay connected me to the distributor in Montréal who he bought music from for his store. They placed a small order of 30 copies. I took the bus to Toronto and went door to door to all the record stores along Yonge Street and Queen Street. I haggled with the shop owners to stock the first release of an independent label they'd never heard of. It was a hard sell. I sold a total of 8 records on that trip.

Trevor yelled out "There it is!" when the fax of new releases came through the Beat Boutique the following week. There was my record, listed among all these artists that I admired. It felt surreal. A few months prior the thought of making my own tracks was just an idea. Now I could hold physical copies in my hand and my music was being listed beside artists I looked up to.

It was as I was sorting through music before a gig that it hit me that most of the records I was playing at the time were from the U.S. and the U.K. They were imports. As it stood, I only had limited domestic distribution. Trying to get my records sold overseas seemed like an impossible feat, but the U.S. market was 10 times the size of Canada's and it was so close.

As I spent more time hanging out in the Toronto record stores, I started asking around about U.S. distributors. Where were they buying their imports and who was a good distributor for the breakbeats I was into? People were tight lipped. Were they concerned I would try and open up a competing record shop or simply wary about sharing info with a young skinny kid in baggy clothes? Who knows. Possibly both.

Several weeks went by but eventually my perseverance paid off when someone working at one of the shops downtown gave me the name and mailing address of a buyer at a well-known music distributor in New York City. Once my second release came out, I mailed a copy to New York and held my breath.

I was mixing music in my bedroom when I heard the sounds of my fax machine behind me. I didn't get faxes often and wasn't expecting anything. It was an order from Nemesis Music Distribution in New York. They wanted 150 copies.

When I called Nemesis to confirm the order and next steps, I couldn't contain myself. I cheered.

"It's just 150 copies," their buyer, Dave, said. I could hear the smile in his voice as he tried to tame my enthusiasm. I didn't care. This was big.

A few weeks barely passed before the second order came through. Nemesis wanted another 200 copies! I was floored. Something Dave had said on that second call struck me, though: "I'd order more if it weren't for the duties we have to pay."

I was ecstatic to be selling records internationally but me being in another country and having the border between us was a hindrance to sales. There was a spark of potential here and I could turn it into a bigger fire if I fanned the flames. How could I get around this? Could I manufacture products in the U.S.? What would be involved? I had way more questions than I had answers.

I made the realization while filling out the customs declaration forms for the shipment of Laidback Lab's fourth release. I had to describe what was in the shipment and check the appropriate box marking whether it was a gift, a sample, a sale, or documents. If I chose "gift" or "sample," the receiver did not have to pay duty on the items received.

What if there was a way to leverage that?

Laidback Lab Records ceased to exist after that fourth release. I shut it down and started a new company called Promo Records in its place. Promotional records, often called promo records or simply "promos," are free copies of new releases, normally shared with influential DJs and music reviewers in advance of the official release date. This is done in hopes of generating buzz for the music before it comes out. With that in mind, Promo Records' tagline became "Every DJ loves a Promo."

What I didn't talk about publicly was the change I made behind the scenes. Whenever I was sending an international shipment with my new company, I marked it as "sample" on the declaration form and wrote "promotional records" in the description box. If customs were to open the boxes and look at the product, the labels clearly said Promo Records. My international sales doubled overnight. The dream of becoming a professional artist that made a living from music was starting to feel real.

Jay in the Beat Boutique on Bayfield Street in Barrie

9

Whoops

"Do you want to drive to Vancouver?"

Jay was asking me a question I'd never been asked before.

"What car are we driving and when are we going?" I asked. I was interested, but had questions of my own.

"My friend moved out there and has landed a great job, but his car is still here and he needs it driven out to him".

"How will we get back?"

"He's going to cover our flights home."

My instinct was to say yes. I'd always wanted

to drive across the country, see the Prairies, the mountains, and the Pacific Ocean.

It sounded like an adventure, but I didn't have much money. I spoke to my parents about it and they gave me $200 and a disposable camera for the trip. They called it a graduation present. Which is funny, given that I had dropped out of high school.

Less than a week later, on a sunny afternoon, we jumped into his friend's little grey Honda CRX and started our journey. The plan was to drive straight there. No hotels and no stops other than gas and food. We wanted to maximize our time in Vancouver. It was a 4,269-kilometre drive from where we were in Ontario. (That's 2,652 miles.) Or put another way, 44 hours of driving if we took *zero* stops.

The challenge? The car had a manual transmission, and other than a few brief experiences previously, I didn't really know how to drive stick shift.

I shared this with Jay. "I can't drive stick shift. Definitely not for a cross-country trip."

"You'll have the hang of it by the time we get to Vancouver," he said. He wasn't wrong.

To achieve our insane driving marathon and do it in the safest way possible, we devised a system. We'd each do driving shifts that were three hours long, then switch. If you were in the passenger seat, you had to stay awake for the first hour and the last hour of the other person's driving stint as that is when they were most likely to be sleepy.

We were on the winding roads of Northern Ontario when it happened. There were trees lining both sides of the two-lane highway, and signs warning drivers to watch out for deer and moose. It was close to 4 a.m., pitch dark, and I was fast asleep. I had passed out with my head resting against the passenger seat window and drool coming out of my mouth when the car suddenly jerked. I woke up to the sound of our wheels skidding onto gravel as Jay tried to regain control of the car.

"Whoops." That's what Jay said as he pulled the car to a stop. He had fallen asleep at the wheel.

"What do you mean 'Whoops?!' It's not a wrong turn. It's not missing an exit. We almost drove off the road!" I shouted. It was rare that I'd talk to Jay in this manner but I was pissed.

We were going to have to change our "no stopping other than for essentials" rule to ensure that we didn't die. We found a safe place to pull over around the next bend. We were somewhere west of Thunder Bay, off the Trans-Canada Highway, in the middle of fucking nowhere. After hours of driving through endless woods and walls of granite that make up the Canadian Shield, we had found ourselves in a clearing. Other than the odd 18-wheeler trucks passing by in the distance, it was quiet.

As I drifted off, I noticed green streaks hovering in the star-filled sky. I rubbed my eyes. Was I dreaming? It was faint at first but got brighter the longer I looked. Holy shit! I was seeing the northern lights. I couldn't believe it. Tears rolled down my cheeks as I admired the green and yellow colours swirling in the sky. I was grateful that we almost drove off the road. Otherwise, I would have missed them altogether.

We didn't sleep long. A couple of hours was all we needed. Plus, trying to force sleeping longer wasn't worth it once the bright sun was up.

By the time we made it to Winnipeg, over 1,900 kilometres later, I wouldn't say that I was smooth at driving stick, but I was no longer grinding the car's gears.

As we pulled back onto the highway after one of our stops for food and gas, we heard a loud metallic thud. Our little car suddenly sounded like an army tank.

We pulled over to investigate. As Jay had suspected, we'd lost the muffler. We weighed our options. We could find a place to get the car fixed and his friend would reimburse us upon arrival, but we had limited money on us, we were on a clock, and a car without a muffler still works, it's just incredibly loud. We could still get to Vancouver safely. We just wouldn't be able to sneak up on anyone.

It's common for people to complain about how boring it is to drive across the flatlands of the Canadian Prairies. I get it. The roads are straight and monotonous, plus the horizon really does seem endless. But there's beauty in contrast and you often need contrast to fully appreciate things. Seeing the Rocky Mountains grow across your horizon is immensely more majestic after that prairie drive.

As we approached the Rockies, what started off as dark specs on the bottom of the skyline slowly grew into mountains that filled our entire field of vision. It soon felt like we were driving in a Bob Ross painting. We rolled down the windows to breathe in the refreshing mountain air. We had made it.

We got into Vancouver two days after leaving Barrie. The total trip had taken us 52 hours door to door.

While Jay and his friend caught up and reminisced over shared stories, I sat and admired Vancouver out of the living room window. We were in the city but the air smelled fresh and a mountain range provided a striking backdrop for all the buildings. I liked the energy here.

Leaving the army base and moving to Barrie had led to me to going on this cross-country adventure. I liked where I was heading.

10

Cliff Jumping

I wasn't overly eager but Jay was interested.

Someone had poured concrete and installed a springboard into the side of a cliff leading into what is essentially the Pacific Ocean, and Jay's friend was selling us on going cliff jumping. I wanted to be excited. I wanted to be adventurous. But I can't say that the details were selling me on it.

"The springboard is about a 60-foot drop to the water," Jay's friend explained. "You can get closer to a 70-foot fall if you let go at the apex of the rope swing. If you climb up a few more rocks and are willing to jump through bushes in a leap of faith, you can get an 85-foot drop. It's wild."

He was eager to take us.

While I wasn't sure that I was going to do the actual jump, I did want to see a springboard into the ocean, so we made our way up the Sea-to-Sky Highway the next day, stopping about 30 minutes outside of Vancouver in a place called Lions Bay. As I stepped out of the car, I imagined what it must be like to live here. Everywhere I looked I saw mansions with big properties and stunning coastal views that were likely worth more than my dad had earned in his entire life.

We had to be covert as we made our way to the cliffs. Getting there meant crossing some private property and walking along train tracks where the RCMP were known to ticket trespassers. It wasn't long until we saw a worn path to the right of us. We had to watch our step as rocks and tree roots made the trail bumpy. As we walked up the final incline, I could hear the ocean waves crashing into the cliffs below.

We got to the top and the view opened up. Suddenly we were standing on the edge of a massive cliff, high above the water. Jagged rock faces lined the other side of the bay in the distance. It didn't matter if I jumped into the ocean or not. This sight alone was worth the trek.

There was a rope swing hanging off of a massive tree branch that leaned out toward the water, and below it was a springboard jutting out of the rocks. As I looked out, I saw what seemed like seals in the distance. Someone who had just made the plunge told us there were whales not far out earlier. British Columbia's licence plate slogan doesn't lie. It is beautiful.

While I had more experience swimming than I did driving standard. I was not a great swimmer. Sure, I went to pools once in a while as a kid. Mostly I just horsed around with my friends. I never took swimming lessons and didn't think highly of my own physical strength.

But everyone else was doing it and seemed to be having a blast. Jay leaped off the springboard and did the rope swing. There were even some crazy people leaping through the bushes above from the third jumping point that Jay's friend had told us about.

"You can do it," Jay said. He sensed that I was hesitant.

When would I ever have this opportunity again? Someone put in a diving board. It had to be safe, right? This is what I was saying to myself as I walked slowly to the edge of the springboard. The sandpaper texture of the board below my feet reminded me of being at the local pool as a kid. I took a deep breath, closed my eyes and leaped off the end. My fear turned to excitement for a brief moment as the wind rushed against my face.

I wasn't in the water long when I knew I was in trouble. No matter how hard I swam, I wasn't getting closer to the rocks. There was an undertow. It was pulling me under and making it hard for me to catch my breath.

Panic set in as I swallowed water and struggled to get air in my lungs. I was getting tired and I was now drifting further from the shore. There were a couple of minutes where I was certain I was going to die. I remember thinking, "This is how I'm going to go? My mom is going to be so disappointed."

As I fought to breathe, adrenalin kicked in. Then I remembered something I had heard when I was a Boy Scout about swimming sideways instead of straight ahead if you were stuck in an undercurrent. I aimed to the left and gave it my all. I made some progress. I turned my body the other way and continued. It seemed to be working. I zigzagged my way back.

Completely exhausted, I pulled myself up onto the flat rocks at the bottom of the cliffs and stayed there for a long while.

"Today is not the day I die," I said out loud to myself. Thankfully, I was more resilient than I thought.

11

Vancouver Local Rate

It was our last day in Vancouver. We were having lunch on an outdoor patio by the water as a steady flow of healthy-looking people were running and biking past us on a nearby path.

I'd fallen in love with the city. It was a metropolis, but it was surrounded by beauty. With the ocean and mountains at its side, it didn't have the frantic energy I sometimes felt when visiting Toronto. People worked to live here, not the other way around. I wanted to come back, but how could I? I was barely able to afford this trip.

I had recently read both *The Celestine Prophecy* and *Think And Grow Rich*. The books were opening me up to the idea that I could be the intentional creator of my life in a new way. It involved putting an aim out into the world without knowing how it would unfold and aligning myself to the feelings of it being true while taking steps toward it.

"I'm going to come back and DJ in Vancouver. I don't know how, but it's going to happen," I said without even thinking.

Jay and his friend looked puzzled.

I had played shows in the smaller cities around Toronto, but this was on the other side of the country. I didn't know anyone involved in the scene here.

The list of reasons why it couldn't happen was long. I didn't spend a drop of energy thinking about those. Once it was declared, I couldn't shake the feeling that it was true. I was going to come back to Vancouver and DJ here, and it was going to be sooner rather than later.

As our plane took off that evening, I looked down at the city below and said "See you soon, Vancouver."

When we got home, I pinned a postcard of Vancouver to the wall above my turntables. I looked at it every time I turned on my equipment to practise. I pictured myself looking up from the turntables knowing that I was playing in Vancouver.

Only a few months had passed when I got an email. The title simply said "Booking Inquiry."

The sender had bought one of my mix tapes at one of the stores I was selling them at in Toronto. He loved the music and wanted to talk to me about playing an event in Vancouver. It felt like magic. How could it be happening this quickly? It wasn't a done deal yet, though. We needed to talk on the phone first. We made arrangements for a call a few days later.

"We'd obviously pay for your flight and accommodations. How much do you want to play? What is your fee?"

An awkward silence followed.

I wasn't ready for that question. I had been vividly imagining myself getting to DJ in Vancouver but hadn't prepared for this obvious and inevitable question.

"What's the going rate for the local DJs there?" I asked, trying to buy myself some time to figure out what the hell I was going to say.

"$150."

"You can pay me that."

My going rate for shows in Ontario was $150 to $200. I could've easily asked for way more—$300, $500? Possibly $750? I was still a relatively unknown artist, but this was an inbound inquiry asking me to come headline an event in another city. *He* had approached *me*.

I was so excited that it was happening that I didn't care about the money. Someone was willing to pay for my flight and all my expenses to perform in Vancouver only months after I set the intention. I almost couldn't believe it.

12
$50 Bonus

Once I got back home from the gig in Vancouver, I continued playing shows in the smaller towns around Toronto while simultaneously trying to make a name for myself in the big city. I got excited when an offer finally came through to play for someone new in Toronto.

It didn't matter that it was for the opening slot in the second room of the event. It was my first time playing for this promoter. They had a reputation for putting on awesome events, and had agreed to pay me $250 to perform. Not only was this a good fee for me as a local DJ at the time, but also I really needed the money.

We showed up before the doors opened at 10 p.m. The lights were still on in the venue as they were doing the final setup with the sound system and decorations. As I put my stuff down in the smaller second room where I was to play, the promoter asked me a question.

"Would you be willing to come back and play at 3:30 a.m. in the main room instead? I'll give you an extra $50 for switching."

That might sound late to you, but you can't get any more prime time for a rave. That's the peak of the party. The early birds haven't left yet, and the late arrivals who come from a pre-party or after the bars have closed are there by then, too.

I tried to play it cool, but I was excited. The side room I was originally booked for held 200 people. The main room I was now going to play in had a capacity of 1000. A year ago I was struggling to break into the Toronto scene. Now I was getting a shot at the main stage.

I had five hours to kill and I knew just the spot. My date and I drove a couple of blocks to System Soundbar. The promoter of the night hooked us up and gave me a handful of drink tickets.

It felt celebratory. We danced, we ordered shots, and between the free drink tickets and a $50 bonus to burn, the drinks flowed.

Last call arrived and I was slurring my words. My date was just as drunk. We stumbled our way out to the car. I got in the driver's seat and without thinking, I drove back to the party venue. I don't remember the drive whatsoever. It's a miracle that I didn't crash or kill anyone. I'm not proud of this.

We got to the parking lot outside the rave and could hear the rumbling of the bass from the music inside. It was 2:30 a.m. I still had an hour until I played. An hour to sober up. I barfed out the window. We both passed out.

I woke up in a daze with a pounding headache. I looked at the clock—it was 4:30 a.m. Shit. I woke up my date, grabbed my bag of records and ran inside. I could still taste the vomit in my mouth. I must have smelled terrible.

I made my way through the crowd to the stage. The party was packed, and the volume of the music was hurting my head. I was sweaty, embarrassed and still drunk. I struggled to talk.

"Where were you?" The promoter asked.

He was pissed. It was too late. Someone else had played in my absence.

I didn't play and I didn't get paid.

Instead of getting my shining moment on a Toronto main stage, I burned a relationship with a supportive promoter and humiliated myself. I had also endangered myself, my date, and countless others by driving drunk.

While I would never again drive after drinking, my struggles with booze were just getting started.

13
Daft Punk

When I was trying to break into the highly competitive music scene in Toronto, I faced a challenge a lot of people face when trying to get work.

That is, you can't get experience without the job but you also can't get the job without experience. With the mega raves in Toronto, you were either on these lineups and you got to play these parties (which meant you got to play more of them), or you were excluded.

I was DJing in cities all over Ontario. I'd been lucky enough to get flown out to play in Vancouver, and I'd even performed at a show in Indiana, but trying to crack into the Toronto scene was hard.

It was particularly challenging because they would print 10,000, 20,000, 30,000, sometimes 40,000 beautiful fold-out glossy flyers for these massive events and they were distributed everywhere. All the promotion further reinforced the divide between those who were on the lineups and those who weren't. You were simply in or you were out.

So I asked myself, "What can I do? What can I do to break through this wall?" I decided to make my own damn flyers. They weren't fancy or glossy but they got people's attention because they said "Who the Fuck Is Robb G?" in bold letters across the top. They had a mini bio about what I'd been doing with music, they had some pictures, and they even listed my shoe size for fun. I printed 15,000 of these things.

I put them in all the cool shops and handed them out outside of parties just like all the event promoters did. Sometimes that meant that I was playing in a neighbouring city until 3 a.m. or 4 a.m. and then driving to Toronto to stand outside handing out flyers as people were leaving events in the wee hours of the morning.

It created such a buzz that my good friend Pat Brown even took the time to create a parody version titled "Who the Fuck Cares?" I still laugh when I think about it now.

The campaign totally worked. Its impact surpassed any possible expectations I had. Within a matter of months I started getting bookings for bigger and better events. Before I knew it, I was on the bill of mega multi-room parties in Toronto, Hamilton, and Niagara Falls, New York, playing alongside top-level international artists that I admired.

Of all the shows I got to play in the 12 months after I started that push, the one I'm most proud of is Syrous' six-year anniversary event. Daft Punk was headlining. My name was all the way at the bottom of the flyer. I was literally the very last artist listed, but I didn't care. It didn't matter. I'd broken through and got to play a party with Daft Punk.

For years to come, and to this day still, people bring up this flyer and the "Who the Fuck Is Robb G?" campaign to me. It makes me smile every single time as it reminds me of how I used creativity and determination to find a way to make things happen, regardless of the odds.

You can lament about all the things you don't have and the resources you're lacking, or you

can work with what you've got and do things differently. You always have a choice.

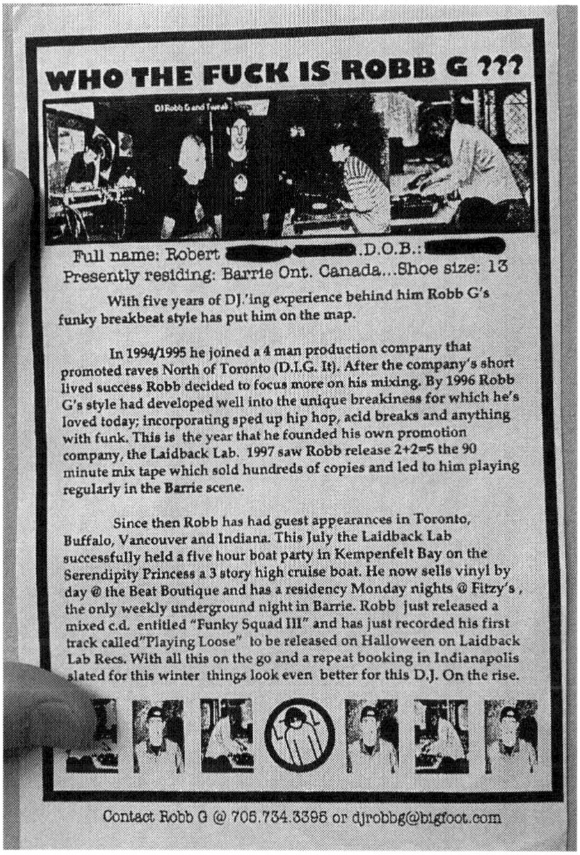

A copy of the "Who The Fuck Is Robb G?" flyer

The flyer for Syrous' six-year anniversary event
"Hyperactive" - September 4th, 1999

14

Watch Me Do Homework

"Do you want to come over and watch me do homework?"

As far as invites to hang out were concerned, it was definitely original. But was she flirting?

I had moved to Toronto to fully pursue my music dream and it had paid off. I was not only playing notable Toronto events but now I was also regularly travelling to other cities to perform. Monika and I ran in similar circles. She was a talented DJ who broke the rules with her creative approach. I loved watching her play. She had short black hair and she was cute. Unlike with other people in the scene where the conversations tended to be superficial, when we ran into each other at parties, we ended up in longer, more engaging discussions about music trends, business ideas, and creativity.

We'd even had a joint birthday party together the previous year when a promoter booked us to play the same night, since our birthdays were one day apart. But we had never hung out outside of a club.

I agreed to come over and went with no expectations. We chatted for a bit and it was clear that she didn't really want to do homework. She wanted a distraction to justify not doing her homework. We decided we'd watch a movie and made our way to Blockbuster where we chose a film called Poolhall Junkies. It was crap. The fact that it was terrible turned out to be good as we talked the entire time instead. It was fun and flirty, but we didn't kiss.

I was off to the U.K. to play some gigs a couple of days later, so a second "homework" session would have to wait. What the flight to London did provide was an opportunity to reflect. As I started writing down what I appreciated about Monika, it unexpectedly turned into a letter. She was smart, creative, and understood music. We seemed to laugh easily when we were in each other's presence and she noticed the absurdity in situations that others missed. I wasn't sure I would give it to her, but it felt good to get it out. While I was running between playing shows, DJing on the radio, and meeting with my European distributor, we exchanged messages on MSN Messenger. I knew I wanted to see her again sooner rather than later and invited her over for dinner. We made plans for the night I got back.

Buzzing on a mix of jet lag and excitement to see Monika, I rushed home from the airport. She came to my place and I made the most elaborate meal I knew how to cook: a shitty vegetarian lasagna. (We were both vegetarian.) I gave her the letter and the date ended with a kiss.

It wasn't long before we were hanging out several times a week. We were dating for less than six months when we decided to live together, and I proposed a few days before we moved into our new apartment. You can say that an invite to watch her do homework quickly evolved into a whole lot more.

15

Without A Paddle

Monika and I had gotten married and she was pregnant with our first child.

With the pressures of adult life starting to mount and a baby on the way, I had to put my music pursuits on hold and start working "real jobs." I ended up in an HR role where the people were nice but I was underpaid, we were understaffed, and the team was underappreciated. My direct manager lacked some key leadership skills. I hated it. I got up every day with a huge knot in my stomach and it was affecting the rest of my life.

The options didn't feel plentiful, but I had to do something. So I started by making a list. If I was going to continue doing office work, what would my next job have? This is the wish list that I came up with:

1. A closer walk to work. (Which was ridiculous because my current walk to work was only 15 minutes.)
2. A $10,000 raise.
3. I'd get to use my bilingualism.
4. It would be in the same industry.
5. I'd work for a supportive leader who I could learn from.

I wrote all these things down and reviewed them morning and night. I created the belief in my gut that this role existed and that I would find it. I started applying to jobs with this vision in mind.

For the first while, nothing happened. I wasn't getting replies and I wasn't getting phone interviews. This went on for several weeks. A month in, I got up one morning and I checked the job boards like I always did. There it was. I saw the role: a bilingual HR position that I was perfectly suited for. I knew absolutely that this was it.

I went into my office that morning and I handed in my resignation, telling my boss that I was quitting because I got hired at the other company. Then I went home at lunch and I applied for the job. That's right—I quit my current role before I'd even applied for the new one. That's how certain I was.

Then the countdown clock was on. I had two weeks to get the job. I'd given my resignation and in two weeks I'd be out of work.

A week and a half passed and nothing happened. When I had only three days left in my role, I got a phone call.

The moment I answered the phone I knew I was in trouble. The recruiter seemed so unenthusiastic about talking with me that it sounded like someone had put a gun to her head and forced her to call me.

She had all kinds of issues with me and was picking my resumé apart for valid reasons. She was giving me a hard time about my lack of formal post-secondary education, and that I'd jumped jobs a bit. I felt it all going downhill.

The phone interview was going terribly and then she asked me: "When you speak in French, do you have an accent?"

As she said it I picked up just a smidge of an East Coast accent.

"Speaking of accents," I said, "I know this has nothing to do with the interview, but I can't help but notice, where on the East Coast are you from?"

Her answer made it clear that she was confused.

"What are you talking about?" she asked.

I doubled down and asked again.

"Where on the East Coast are you from?"

"Truro."

I couldn't believe it. I was born in Truro. It's a 10,000 person town, if that, half a country away.

The recruiter then started talking about the family business that her parents had there. I shared how my grandmother lived just outside of town and the memories I had of visiting Truro as a child.

The moment I told her where I was born, her tone of voice and demeanour completely changed. Our conversation ended with her saying, "You come in tomorrow morning and we'll talk about how we're going to get you this job."

I went in the next day. It wasn't a formal interview. We just talked about how she could get me in front of the hiring manager. She said the hiring manager would be reluctant to meet me and would have the same kind of objections she did. So I asked her, "Do you want to fill this job?" She said yes. "Do you think I can do it?" She said yes again.

"Get me in front of the hiring manager and I guarantee you that I'll get the job." I said it with complete unwavering confidence.

A couple of days later was my last day at work. At the going away party, I got a paddle signed by the entire department of 30 people because they said when I started "They were up the creek without a paddle."

I got an interview with the hiring manager early the following week. It went tremendously well and ran almost twice as long as it was scheduled for. At the end of the meeting she said, "Look, I've been in HR for over 20 years and I would never do this kind of thing. But if I would offer you a job on the spot, how soon could you start?"

I got the job and it met every single thing on my list. It was a closer walk to work, and I was working for a wonderful person. It was in the same industry, and I was going to get to use my bilingualism. It fell short just slightly in one area: I didn't get a $10,000 raise. I only got an $8500 raise. I was quite content with that.

The craziest part of all this? The recruiter from Truro who was instrumental in making this all line up? She'd already given her notice and was leaving for another job. Two weeks after I started the new gig, she was gone.

16

12 Inch Therapy

I'd been to the annual Miami music conference a couple of times. I'd met people, heard good music, and partied, but I can't say that it had done much to move the needle for my record label business or DJ career.

With some new music coming out that I was feeling enthusiastic about, I wanted to give the event another go. Monika and I both needed a vacation and we decided to make a road trip out of it. I booked a week off work, reserved a rental car, and we made arrangements for our now 18-month-old daughter to stay with Monika's parents.

One of the new pieces of music I was excited about was a song called "12 Inch Therapy." My old friend Sheldon, who had helped me write some of my very first songs, had engineered it for me.

The funny track name was an homage to the fact that 12-inch vinyl records were finally dying off in the DJ world. The advent of digital DJ interfaces and CD players that looked like and acted like a turntable were finally ending the vinyl record reign in the DJ industry.

Leading up to the trip, I sent out advanced copies to a handful of influential artists who I thought might be into the song, hoping to try and spark some pre-conference buzz. I hadn't heard anything back from anyone.

With the car all packed and ready to go, Monika ran back up to the apartment to switch jackets before we left. She'd decided that she would be better off with a lighter coat. Our destination had palm trees.

There was no traffic leaving the city and we made awesome time. We got to Windsor, the Canadian city on the other side of Detroit, in just over three hours. We pulled off the highway at a rest stop to hit the washrooms and grab a bite before crossing the border.

We were stepping out of the car when I saw the look of horror on Monika's face.

"What is it?'

"My wallet and all my ID are in the other jacket."

I got out of the car without saying a word. Monika stayed in the passenger seat.

We were going to have to drive more than six hours only to be in the same goddamn spot we were in right now. I belted out a string of Québecois profanity at the top of my lungs as I stormed around the gravel parking lot kicking rocks.

"Maudit calice osti tabarnak!"

When I'm really upset, I swear in French.

Once I ran out of rocks to kick and swear words to say, I got back in the car. Monika quietly said she was sorry. She was hesitant to say more. It was an extremely quiet ride for the next hour. No music. No conversation.

When my blood pressure dropped back to normal levels, I began reflecting on what had happened.

Did she intend to forget her wallet and make us drive an extra six hours? No. She clearly felt bad. I realized that me staying mad wasn't going to change a thing. All it would do would make the rest of the drive miserable for both of us and we had a long drive ahead of us. **We tend to judge ourselves based on our intentions and others based on their actions. It's a recipe for conflict and resentment.**

"Thanks for apologizing. I'm sorry I got so mad."

"I understand, I'd be pissed too."

"You obviously didn't intend to forget your wallet and I don't want this to ruin the rest of the trip."

Monika put music on and we were laughing about the incident not long after. When we got back to the same rest stop in Windsor six hours later, we cheered.

Highlights of the rest of the journey down include sketchy men in a beat-up Ford Tempo offering to sell us a used laptop "in great condition" on the side of the highway, and the comedic struggle to find vegetarian food options in the state of Georgia.

"Do you have anything vegetarian?" we asked the hostess at one restaurant.

"Sure, the salads."

We looked at the salads on the menu. All three had meat. One of them had both chicken *and* bacon. So much for that.

Once in Miami, we checked into our hotel and made our way to one of the pool parties where several artists I knew were playing.

The party was packed with dozens of huge artists from all over the world. I had some CD copies of 12 Inch Therapy with me and had tried giving them out to a few of the bigger name DJs. The responses ranged from outright disinterest to going through the motions of saying "Thanks" before chucking it into their bag with dozens of other promos they'd already received.

One of the artists at the event was DJ Icey, an American rave pioneer and legend in the world of breakbeat music. We'd met a few times before and were on a first name basis already, but that didn't change the fact that I saw him as an idol. I'd been buying and playing his records since the mid '90s. His music had had a profound impact on me.

"Got your 12 Inch Therapy tune and dig it," is what he said to me after I walked up to shake his hand and say hello.

"Yeah?"

"I'm going to play it today."

I was standing behind DJ Icey when he dropped my song in the middle of his set. The reaction was instant. Moments later, several well-known artists were at the DJ booth asking the same question.

"What the hell is this?"

People who had brushed me off an hour before were suddenly asking me if I could hook them up with a copy.

12 Inch Therapy was played at every major event at the conference, including Ultra Music Festival, which had 50,000 people in attendance that year. At one 3000 person club event, it was played by two headlining acts in a row—one played the original and the other played the remix, by Australian artist Bass Kleph.

By the time we left Miami, everyone was talking about the song and everyone who didn't have a copy wanted one.

12 Inch Therapy, and the remix in particular, exploded.

This included:

- Topping underground music charts
- Receiving rave reviews in multiple leading

U.K. music magazines (including being called "track of the year" in one of them)

- Being licensed to a big Ministry of Sound compilation in Australia
- Becoming the #1 requested and #1 played song for the *entire year* on a SiriusXM radio channel.

It's hard to grasp the domino effect this song and its impact had on my life. From helping me to get regular guest DJ spots on SiriusXM radio to opening the door for me to play at multiple new events and festivals, it laid the foundation to create the momentum I needed to leave my office job and focus full-time on music again.

17

Shambhala

It was an all-ages bash, at a venue known for its sketchy after-hours parties, and the place was only about half full when I got there. Not what you'd call the scene for a life-changing event to occur. "Every gig counts" was a motto I lived by so I ignored those details, focused on the eager people who were there, and poured my heart into my performance.

What I didn't know was it was someone in the crowd's first party. Their older brother had taken them out dancing, and my set made a lasting impression on them. His name was Jesse and he was going to help spark a career-changing moment for me.

Set in the Kootenays region of beautiful British Columbia, an area described as a "mountain playground with enormous snowy peaks, clear lakes, and waterfalls" on the official tourism website, Shambhala is a one of a kind music festival that takes place every summer. Its six stages are living works of art that evolve year after year, as the event has been on the same farm for more than two decades.

The Village stage has treetop ramps high above the crowd, reminiscent of an Ewok Village. Another stage is set on a beach by a river, where attendees dance in the sand. All of the stages prioritize delivering out of this world visual and auditory experiences where visitors can soak in bass while dancing surrounded by artwork. Those attending the event tend to wear elaborate costumes and are some of the friendliest humans you'll ever meet. It's magical.

So what did Jesse do? He made it his life's mission to get me booked at Shambhala. He went on the festival's message board and regularly posted my name under the "What acts do you want to see at Shambhala" thread. He shared links to my sets, plugged my releases, and personally spoke to one of the stage managers, Rich.

Sure, I was now making music and DJing full time and had some tracks out that were doing well, but Jesse, the best hype man an artist could ever ask for, made it happen. When the booking inquiry came through, I knew that the gig could be monumental for my career, assuming I didn't screw it up.

I'd heard stories and seen pictures, but nothing could've prepared me for the actual event.

"Where the fuck am I?!"

That was DJ Nu-Mark, one of the artists riding with me in the shuttle from the airport. He was trying to process what we were seeing as we pulled into the festival grounds. We'd just driven past someone in a full-body lion costume blowing oversized bubbles, and a topless woman in blue body paint hula hooping.

I was scheduled to play extremely late Saturday night from 5:30 a.m. to 7:30 a.m. in the Fractal Forest. I was worried about performing at that hour but the stage manager, Rich, assured me that it would be great.

As I walked up the stairs of the stage for my set, I stood in awe. The Fractal Forest's DJ booth was built into the trunk of a hollowed out 30-foot-wide old-growth tree stump with a large pyramid shaped roof hanging above. It was a visual spectacle, set under a lush tree canopy. A 360-degree immersive experience with hundreds of people surrounding the stage on all sides. I watched as dozens of lights, lasers, and video projections bathed the trees, the massive funky wooden art, and the dancing crowd in a colourful glow.

While my senses absorbed my surroundings, my heart rate began to increase and my breath got shallower. Malente, a talented DJ from Germany, was playing before me and absolutely smashing it. I had DJed countless places before and had loads of unreleased music that I was excited to play, but I was nervous. This was a big deal.

Then I noticed the equipment was in an unusual setup. The CD players were mounted higher up on a secondary platform away from the mixer. I could make it work, but it would be awkward. I thought about not saying anything but I decided to speak up. I wanted the best environment for my set.

I got the sound guy's attention and let him know I needed the CD decks moved. He closed his eyes so I wouldn't see them roll and shook his head.

"They're fine where they are," he replied. It was late. He was tired. And he didn't want to go through the trouble of rearranging everything. I insisted.

"I need them on the same level to be able to play," I said.

I wasn't going to budge. He reluctantly reconfigured the equipment setup.

The crowd was still going strong as Malente was finishing up. I couldn't believe how many people were there at 5:30 a.m. I plugged in my headphones, took three deep breaths, and went to work. Malente patted me on the back, wished me a good set, and mentioned he was tired and would be leaving shortly.

What happened over the next two hours was nothing short of a spiritual experience. Feeling guided by intuition, I played new music that I didn't intend to play. Following hunches, I found perfect mixes of tracks I had never previously layered together. My hands moved as if someone else was controlling them. The music flowed through every cell in my body. I screamed at the crowd and they screamed back.

Festival staff danced on the speakers in front of me and artists from around the world gathered behind me. As my last song was ending, I cut the music and yelled "THANK YOUUUUU!!!!!!!" as loud as I could. I was shaking from exhaustion as I put my headphones down. With nothing left in me, I fell over into a ball on the floor completely drained.

The sun was up by the time I was done. Rich, the stage manager, said there were even more people there at the end of my set than when I started. He had never seen anything like that before.

As people hugged and thanked me, I noticed that Malente was still there. He had stayed for my entire set.

While I was gathering my stuff, the sound guy came over.

"I'm sorry I gave you a hard time earlier. I didn't know you were going to do *that*," he said.

I thanked him and let him know I understood.

I had made it. I was a full-time artist and had just played one of the best sets of my life on a stage that I couldn't have designed in my dreams. It was magic. The crowd had gone off to loads of unreleased music of both my own and other artists I had signed to my label. I was soaring and on top of the world.

According to reviews in the local paper and on message boards the following week, I played "one of the highlight sets of the entire festival."

Thanks to that Shambhala performance, I got asked to play all over the West Coast. I can attribute dozens of shows in multiple cities back to that one wild night. I formed bonds with artists and industry people that weekend who would become close friends and influential to my music career. Much of it thanks to Jesse.

Every gig counts. You never know who is in the audience, how you might affect their life, or how they might transform yours.

DJing in San Francisco in 2010

18

KK Papa

"It's KK Papa."

My two-year-old daughter was doing her best to console me with her limited vocabulary. It was just the two of us at home in our small apartment as her mom was out at work. I was supposed to be taking care of her. Instead, she was rubbing my back with her little hands, trying to soothe me as I held the toilet, violently puking.

"It's KK Papa."

I had DJed at a club called Footwork the night before. Known internationally as a hub for underground electronic music, the Toronto venue had a custom sound system, a hidden back alley entrance that made it feel exclusive, and a loyal crowd that loved to dance.

When you're an entertainer, the drinks are free. It's part of your pay. People go out dancing and drinking to forget about their soul-sucking jobs and their problems with their partners. When you're the entertainment, you're expected to fuel the party. Lead the way.

You could say I didn't grow up with the best role models when it came to drinking. While they were responsible, hard-working men, both my grandfathers were alcoholics. Same goes for my pops. He's not one to miss work, take sick days, or skip responsibilities, but a day doesn't pass without him getting drunk. Trying to express concern to my dad about his alcohol abuse never went well. He'd shut down the conversation instantly and say it was "none of your business."

Daily booze consumption wasn't my thing. But from the first time classmates and I got wasted on a swamp water mix of spirits stolen from our parents' liquor cabinets in Grade 7, when I broke the seal, it was all or nothing. Having two drinks and calling it a night is not something I knew how to do. If you would've asked me, I would've said I drank to let loose. I drank to celebrate. I might have even responded that I drank to take the edge off before performing.

A more truthful answer would've been that I drank to feel strong and confident. I drank to silence the voice in my head that loved reminding me of how weak and worthless I was.

This means that I've shamefully cleaned my own barf off the outside of a cab while the driver yelled that I was pathetic. I've had a boss take an awkward call from a client about my behaviour at a work-related event. I've woken up in a daze at 5 a.m. on a club's couch with a man screaming at me because of things I couldn't remember. I've had friends stay the night in my hotel room as they worried whether I might drown in my own vomit. It's not a good list.

I'd become a master at playing down how bad it was. Choosing instead to spin the stories into funny tales to share with friends for laughs. This let me pretend that it wasn't a problem. It was normal. The reality is that there are too many nights where I embarrassed myself, upset friends, offended others, and hurt people because of my drinking.

As my nostrils burned from the stomach acid passing through my nose, the joy of the previous night's festivities was clashing with my daytime role as a dad. My skull was throbbing, my stomach sore from hurling, and now I was crying out of embarrassment as my toddler tried to comfort me.

I was no stranger to feeling self-disgust due to alcohol. However, having my concerned two-year-old daughter take care of me while I puked was a new low. There are countless times when I said "That's it! I'm going to quit drinking!" but it never lasted more than a week.

Friends and peers knew me as someone who drank heavily, got rowdy, and had crazy stories about the recent shenanigans I had stirred. That meant people bought me drinks, egged me on, and expected it of me. It was my identity.

This "drunk Robb" identity was now clashing hard against my determination to be a good father. Something had to change.

I went 30 days without having a drink after that remorseful morning with my daughter. It might not seem like long, but I had been regularly binge drinking for more than 15 years at that point. And working in music meant I was in bars, in nightclubs, and at events several nights a week.

This wouldn't be the last time that I took an extended break from drinking.

19

The Seizure

Our family grew to four with the birth of our son Sébastien and we moved to a bigger apartment to make room for everyone.

He hadn't been feeling well one afternoon so the little dude was napping on the couch when his big sister Sophie, who was now almost five, yelled out for me.

"Papa, there's something wrong with Sébastien!"

Her tone scared me more than her words. My daughter is always calm, unless she sees blood. I could tell by the sound of her voice that she was panicking, and it got my adrenalin pumping before I even entered the room.

There wasn't blood, but I knew something was dangerously off the moment I saw his little body jerking in violent spasms.

I picked him up and his body went stiff as he convulsed in my arms. He was unresponsive to my words and his eyes had rolled into the back of his head. I had no idea what was causing it, but it was clear that my two-year-old son was having some kind of seizure.

"Sophie, go get the phone. Quickly," I said.

As my daughter ran to the other room to grab our cordless phone, I held Sébastien while drool rolled out of his mouth.

"911, what's your emergency?"

After doing my best to describe what was happening, the 911 operator started asking me questions.

"Is he epileptic?"

No.

"Has he had seizures before?"

No.

"Is he responding to your words?"

"No."

Fuck.

I reminded myself to breathe, and the voice on the phone walked me through what to do next with Sébastien's now limp body.

Lay him on his side in the recovery position. Support his head and tilt it back with his chin lifted to ensure he can breathe. Extend one leg out, bent at the knee in a 90-degree angle. Check that nothing is blocking his airway, and loosen any tight clothing.

They stayed on the phone with me until the ambulance arrived.

"I have to commend you for being so calm," said the operator who had guided me through everything.

"Thanks. It's the only thing I can control right now," I replied.

There was no time for panic, no time for what-ifs. I'd make time for that later.

For now, I had to stay alert and focused. Plus, my daughter was looking to me for how to handle the situation. If I remained calm, she would too.

I got a similar series of questions from the paramedics as I had got on the phone while they checked Sébastien's vital signs.

Now that I was done with 911, I could call my wife while the EMTs tended to Sébastien.

"What?! What do you mean? What happened?" she asked. She started crying. Then screaming. I felt her panic in every bone of my body. She was feeling and saying everything that I couldn't.

Sophie and I rode in the back of the ambulance to the hospital with a quiet and subdued Sébastien lying sprawled out on a stretcher. Sophie's excitement about our unique ride was a welcome distraction to the situation.

At the hospital, the nurses descended on us first. Then the doctors. They asked dozens of questions while running Sébastien through tests, bloodwork, and scans.

Hours passed while we waited for the various results. Was anyone in the family epileptic? If it *was* epilepsy, what was the treatment? What if the seizure had caused permanent damage? It was a challenge to stop my mind from wandering into worst case scenarios.

The nurse gave Sophie some crayons and a picture to colour in while we waited. Sophie laughed because all they had to colour were images of Christmas wreaths even though it was summer. While I was happy to see her smiling and I agreed that it was silly, I couldn't laugh.

The head doctor walked back into the room holding forms in a folder. They had news.

"The scans have come back clear. He's going to be OK," the doctor said.

She continued talking but everything she said after those initial words sounded muffled. Nothing registered as my shoulders dropped and I let out a full body sigh.

"Sorry, could you repeat that?"

"He had a febrile seizure. It's common in young children with a fever as their bodies don't have the same ability to regulate their temperature."

"Does this mean he has epilepsy? Will he have more seizures?" I asked.

"He has a slightly higher risk of developing epilepsy but it's not common. He is however at risk of having more febrile seizures in the next couple of years if he's sick and running a temperature."

Sensing I needed to hear it a second time, she

repeated, "He's going to be OK."

I quietly made my way to a bathroom stall down the hall, locked the door, and cried. It was loud. It was ugly. It was a relief.

It didn't matter what else I had going on. All I could think about was Sébastien and Sophie. My kids were everything to me.

20

Affording It

"The only reason we're still married is I can't afford the divorce."

Have you ever regretted the words you were saying even before they were done leaving your mouth?

I don't even remember what Monika and I were fighting about. It doesn't matter because it had nothing to do with what we were discussing and everything to do with what we weren't talking about.

My words hurt. Monika went from yelling at me to a stunned silence. She left the living room without saying another word.

It was unusual for us to have this kind of argument. We rarely fought. That's not because things were all peachy. It's because we didn't talk about the important stuff.

That approach can work in the short term but ignoring things for extended periods only builds pressure and leads to an eventual larger outburst. It's kind of like ignoring the snow on your sidewalk in the winter. If you shovel it when the snow is fresh, it's easy to clear out and you can regain a clear path rather easily. However, if you ignore the snow and don't address it, when there's a change in temperature, it will harden and turn into ice. Then your path will be slippery, dangerous to walk across, and much harder to clear.

Communication in a relationship is much the same as snow: If you don't address stuff when it's fresh, it will build up. Then when the temperature of the relationship changes, it hardens and becomes much harder to discuss or clear.

So what weren't we talking about?

- We were stressed about our unpredictable financial situation since both of us were simultaneously pursuing entrepreneurial paths.
- While I helped a lot with the kids when I was home, I would regularly be out of town

for work, was often away several times each month, and the solution for me to bring in more money was to play more gigs. In other words, be away from home even more.

- When I was in Toronto, I would often be out late either playing local gigs or hanging with out of town artists that were passing through.
- Regardless of whether I was in another city or out late back at home, my life revolved around music, partying, having fun, and getting drunk while Monika stayed home with the kids.
- Unless it was for a family obligation or she managed to come along to one of my DJ gigs, we no longer did things as a couple or spent time together.
- There was no intimacy left in our relationship. Not just physical intimacy, but also intellectual and emotional intimacy.

We used to brainstorm businesses together, share music, go on road trips, confide in each other about the things that scared us, and express our appreciation for one another. Not anymore.

Our relationship had been bumpy for a while, but this was the first time one of us had used the word divorce.

I apologized for saying it, but the damage was done. An apology didn't matter because the important things didn't change: I didn't acknowledge how difficult it was for her to be home with the kids while I was out all the time, and I didn't show my appreciation for all that she did for the kids and the family. I didn't invest time in us or the relationship, change my drinking and partying habits, or share what I was afraid of or show my vulnerability.

Without those changes, the outcome was predictable. It was simply a matter of time.

21

Get Out of Here

My head was pounding, my mouth was dry, and a man with a red face and veins bulging out of his neck was yelling at me.

I didn't recognize him but I gathered from his all-black outfit that he worked at the bar where I played earlier that night, only now he was extremely upset.

"I'll knock your fucking lights out!" he shouted.

Why did this man want to knock me unconscious? I had no idea. It was 5 a.m. and I had just woken up on a sticky fake leather couch in the back room of a nightclub. Whatever I had done earlier in the night to make this man so furious was unknown to me. I couldn't remember.

I was living my high school dream of working as a full-time DJ and music producer. I was being paid to create music while being flown to different cities to perform. Two decades and hundreds of shows later, my passion for sharing music had taken me to heights that I had not dared dream of. I got to bring my sounds to cities across North America and even to a couple in Europe. I got to remix not one but two of my absolute favourite teenage records. I opened for The Prodigy as well as played at Ultra Music Festival, Shambhala, and Burning Man.

And yet, while the party life might have looked incredible to some from the outside, by 2012, I was utterly lost.

The rise of electronic dance music (EDM) in the late 2000s was divisive in the scene. The explosion in popularity of the bubble gum and pop side of the music meant there were new people pouring into a music scene that had been on a steady decline since the rave peak of the '90s. All the new faces meant new clubs, new promoters, and new festivals were sprouting up in every city.

While it's said that a rising tide lifts all boats, with the surge in popularity came loads of people who only started attending because it was the "cool new thing." This new wave, and the billions of dollars in corporate money that came with it, put much less of a focus on the art of DJing and way more emphasis on appearance, choreographed light shows, and social media popularity.

The influx of new people was great for me initially. It meant more gigs and increased rates. In cities where I used to play a smaller club on a Thursday or Friday, I was now being invited to play a new spot in town on the Saturday for a considerably higher fee. But it came at a cost. The venues and events I normally played at were filled with either people who came specifically to hear me or who were open-minded to whatever I would dish their way. There was trust in me as an artist.

By comparison, these new crowds were used to being spoon-fed hits. They wanted to hear top 40 EDM songs that they knew. It wasn't long before I found myself playing music I didn't like, to people who I didn't feel connected to, for a paycheque. I might as well have been a jukebox.

I was no longer hunting for new music to excitedly share with friends. I wasn't making and playing music from the heart anymore. It was all being done to chase a payday. The effects of this loss of purpose in pursuit of money aren't surprising: I was burned out, bummed out, and deeply depressed. But I had a family to feed and needed the money, so I dealt with it the easiest and most acceptable way. I got wasted. A lot.

As a performer, alcohol wasn't simply free—binge drinking was normal and often encouraged. Drinking until I blacked out was no longer an exception. It was becoming the norm.

My mental health and personal relationships were paying the biggest price. My marriage was ending. I hated myself, and the little voice in my head reminded me of this often. Something had to change.

Soon after the incident with the shouting man, I announced my retirement and booked a final tour called "Get Out of Here." It was a string of shows across a handful of cities with a final hurrah at Footwork in Toronto. While the outpouring of support was heartwarming, one comment on the Facebook post I made about my retirement stood out: "You can't retire, that's who you are."

The flyer for my retirement party at Footwork

22

Suicide

Before putting the belt around my neck, I inspected its quality. Was it going to be strong enough to hold my weight?

I'd been crying uncontrollably for days—so much so that it physically hurt to shed tears. I hadn't slept properly in weeks. I struggled to focus.

I had reached the point where cross-armed hugging myself was no longer providing any comfort. Out of desperation and exhaustion I found myself hitting my head on the wall, hoping it would make the agony go away. I had never felt pain like this before. I had to make it stop.

My search history that week included:

- Quickest way to kill yourself
- How to poison yourself
- How to tie a noose

After months of trying to make it work, Monika and I agreed to split. I was sleeping in our spare room and desperately looking for both work and an apartment. The few apartments I could afford had turned me down because I couldn't provide proof of employment. I had a handful of DJ gigs left as part of my retirement tour and needed a job to afford a place to live.

Walking away from an 18-year career in music while processing the end of a marriage was proving to be a deadly combo. Who was "Robb" if I wasn't "Robb G" who made and played music? It's what I'd been doing since high school. Music is how I met my friends. It's how I made money. It's where I'd met my wife. It was my entire identity.

While that spun my head, failing at marriage was crushing my heart. Not only was I losing my best friend, but I also equated failing at marriage with completely and utterly failing as a parent.

My kids were so young and so innocent. How could I let them down like this?

I was a total failure.

Having made the decision to put an end to things the night before, I felt a calm as I woke up one morning. I had a plan and the acceptance of it all was giving me peace. While I'd been in the habit of checking my email first thing in the morning to see if I had any messages about the jobs I had been applying to, on this day I didn't bother. It didn't matter anymore.

Once everyone was gone and the house was empty, I brought a chair to the bottom of the stairs. I put the belt through the buckle, and tied the loose end firmly to the banister above it. I stood on the chair and started to put the belt loop over my head.

As I felt the leather belt around my neck, I was hit with a flash of clarity: If I took my life, all I was going to do was pass on this overwhelming pain I was drowning in to my kids.

And they sure as hell wouldn't know how to deal with it.

The thought of Sophie and Sébastien made me loosen the belt. I slowly stepped down off the chair and sat with my head in my hands. I was crying again but this time it was out of relief.

It's scary to realize how close I was.

23

Going Viral

I looked over my shoulder and saw that my cubicle mate and co-worker was surfing Reddit. I was deathly afraid that he was going to click the third item on the site's front page. It was a link to a video of me.

"Robb G finally made it big."

That was a comment online in response to the video of me going viral.

We're talking over one million views on YouTube and reaching the front pages of Reddit, Gawker, and BuzzFeed. The clip was included in countless "DJ Fails" compilation videos, and Tosh.0 even did a segment on it where he called me "DJ Cranky Pants." It was ALL OVER the Internet.

The incident captured in the 18-second clip happened in 2007 but only came out in 2012 because I was retiring from DJing. I didn't even know the footage existed.

The couple of weeks where the video blew up were some of the weirdest in my life. Every day I was flooded with texts from friends, emails from people I hadn't spoken to in years, and messages in every DM inbox I had online.

After some desperate searching in the months after Monika and I had split and I had announced my retirement from DJing, I finally landed a job as a recruiter thanks to my bilingualism and experience in HR. It had allowed me to move out and get my own place. But being back in the office world meant I was also stressed about co-workers coming across the video that was going viral. They didn't even know I used to DJ. If they saw this clip, it could easily get me fired.

The problem? It was a video of me totally losing my shit, yelling at somebody while DJing.

What you don't see in the video is that a girl had come up to me and was harassing me while I was playing. She was upset that I wasn't paying enough attention to her and her friend dancing on stage. The first time she started rubbing herself on me and yelling in my ear, I was very polite. The second time I was firm and told her I'd be rude if there was a third time. What you see in the video is the third and final time she started touching me. I was at the tail end of a layered three-minute mix with both volumes at 10 and she came over, pulled on my headphone cord and yelled at me. That's when I lost it.

As the years passed I've realized that what makes the incident worse is that I called the person harassing me a slut. It doesn't matter what the woman was doing, or that the incident happened so many years ago. That word has been used to enforce a double standard and shame women into conformity for decades.

Fortunately, my cubicle mate didn't click on the Reddit link and the buzz around the clip eventually died down. Either my co-workers didn't end up seeing the video as it was making its rounds or they didn't realize it was me thanks to the grainy footage. That wouldn't stop the clip from complicating my chances with a future job, though.

24

Begging and Pleading

"It declined."

The rejection she uttered wasn't nearly as embarrassing as when my credit card was declined while I was buying groceries, but having a cashier half your age tell you your card didn't go through always sparks a certain level of shame.

My mattress was no longer on the floor of my apartment as I had finally got a bed frame, but there was still nothing on the walls of my new place. I was trying to decorate. The goal was to make my small 540-square-foot one-bedroom apartment feel more like a home than a bachelor pad. I had fought to get joint custody of the kids and they were about to start living with me half the time.

It wasn't a fancy painting. Heck, it wasn't even really a painting. It was a print. I loved the colours and something about the circles spoke to me.

But I was in debt to the tune of $28,000 and I was going further into the hole every month. I wasn't making enough money to cover my living expenses.

I pretended to act surprised that my card was declined and told the cashier that I'd be right back. I went to the back of the store and spoke quietly on the phone with the credit card company. I was asking for a $50 limit increase, but they weren't willing to do it.

"Unfortunately, I've reviewed your file and you're too high risk," the person on the line said.

I pleaded with them. I told them that I desperately needed it.

"I'm sorry. There's nothing I can do, sir."

"Please."

There was no more hiding the emotion in my voice. I was begging now.

There was a long pause.

"OK, but you really have to get better at making your minimum payments on time and bring down your balance so that you're not constantly at your limit."

"Thank you. You have no idea how much this means to me," I said, and I meant it.

I took a few extra minutes before going back to the cashier to pay for it. I used the time to take deep breaths, lower my heart rate, and gather myself.

When I got home I promptly put the print up directly across from the couch where it couldn't be missed. It was the focal point of the room when you were sitting down. I sat there admiring it for a long time that first night.

It was a symbol that my small apartment was becoming a home for the kids and I. It sat in the background while we watched movies together, and acted as the backdrop behind our little Christmas tree that year.

That picture now hangs behind my desk on my office wall. It's in the background of all the video calls with my coaching clients, and it's in many of the videos I post online. It's there to remind me of when things were different.

25

Halloween Tuxedo

It was the first Halloween since Monika and I had separated and I had moved out. The plan was to meet up with Monika and the kids and we'd all go out trick-or-treating together, like we always had. I was feeling a bit off on my way over. It felt weird whenever I went back to the old apartment.

On my way there, I reflected on why I enjoyed Halloween so much.

It's a day when you can be creative, express yourself, and step out of your usual comfort zones. A holiday where you don't have to stay stuck in your current circumstances.

You can be a fictional character, express your repressed sexual freedom, or have superpowers. You don't have to be who your family, church, friends, community, teachers, or co-workers expect you to be. Halloweeen is liberating.

Like most kids, Sophie and Sébastien looked forward to Halloween. Getting to play dress up with a group of friends while collecting a bag of treats—how can you go wrong? Our place was typically a rendezvous point for our friends and their kids. We'd all go trick-or-treating together in our neighbourhood and then gather back at our apartment to chat and hang out while the kids sorted their loot.

Sophie in particular spends considerable time thinking about her costumes and who she'll be on Halloween. This isn't something that's done in the weeks leading up to the event, either. She'll ask you in the month of November what you're going to dress up as for *next* Halloween because it's already on her mind.

Beyond the fun shared experiences with my kids, I also have a Halloween bond with my pops. He loved Halloween. He wasn't one to celebrate his birthday the day before, on October 30th, but he made up for it on Halloween.

I was in Grade 4 the first year he went beyond handing out candy from a bowl. He took a pair of his work coveralls and stuffed them with scrunched up newspaper to create a full body dummy that he tied to a rope. He then hid in the shadows of the small roof that covered the front steps of our house, suddenly dropping down the dummy as unsuspecting trick-or-treaters walked up to the door.

I cut my own trick-or-treating short that night so I could spend more time watching him chuckle as he scared the shit out of the neighbourhood kids and their parents. I wasn't used to him being around the house and had never heard him laugh so much before.

It became his thing. He started collecting decor and props throughout the year. Like Sophie, he was thinking about next Halloween in November. Every year he added to the experience and it wasn't long until our family owned a collection of giant spiders, tomb stones, multiple albums of eerie music, and a smoke machine.

At its peak, he had a full haunted maze that went through our garage on the side of the house and through our backyard. As I outgrew my own trick-

or-treating, I became a part of his creation, hiding in the maze to spook people as they came through. This Halloween tradition was often the only quality time he and I spent together.

Now I was headed to my old place to spend quality time with my kids on Halloween. I arrived at Monika's dressed up in a tuxedo morph suit and top hat. A morph suit is a full body one piece spandex outfit. They're fun to wear and I felt like a superhero on his way to a fancy dinner party.

The kids greeted me when I walked in. They were already dressed up and excited. Monika complimented me on my costume as she was pulling together odds and ends to whip together an outfit for herself.

"I've got an idea," she said.

She went into the bedroom. I could hear some shuffling down the hall but had no clue what she was up to.

Nothing could've prepared me for what happened next. She came back into the room wearing her wedding dress. I hadn't seen her in it since the night we got married. Our wedding ceremony had been outdoors in the courtyard of a beautiful historical building with 30 of our closest family and friends.

Now Monika was standing in that same dress, in what used to be my living room, seven years later, our broken marriage known to all. She knew it was bold and was waiting for my reaction.

Stunned, I stood in silence.

"I think I'll cover my face and the front of the dress in fake blood. What do you think?" she asked.

"It's hilarious and awesome," I said.

We were the Halloween groom and dead bride.

The kids thought it was funny. They were happy that their separated parents had a couple's costume.

Our friends and neighbours had mixed reactions. I think it was a little much for some of them. I guess a divorce is not supposed to be fun or playful. The ones who got it, absolutely loved it. As one friend put it: "You and Monika are inspiring. You're really setting a different example for what a divorce can be like."

It was both symbolic and cathartic for us. The marriage was dead but we were still a duo, connected by the kids and working together.

26

Celebrate Mondays

Years before, when I took my first ever office job in HR, I had a cubicle desk near the floor kitchenette. It meant that I heard everything discussed between co-workers while they were grabbing a mid-morning tea or rinsing out their lunch tupperware.

Before getting that office gig, all I had known was working in fast-food and retail jobs, being a customer service rep in a call centre, and running my own businesses. This had been my first exposure to adults making a living as career office people.

The only thing more annoying than the cheery "happy Friday" salutations colleagues gave each other as they refilled their coffees, was people celebrating "baby Friday." That's what you call Thursday when you're stuck in a meaningless job you despise and your life revolves around living for the weekend.

It's not that I absolutely adored that first cubicle job, but I knew from experiencing my dad's Sunday night dread as a kid that I had no intention of ever subscribing to the "being miserable on Mondays" mindset. You could set your watch to my dad's mood change on Sunday evenings as his anxiety about returning to work set in. It was predictable. He was an Ammunition Technician in the army. He loved being an expert on explosives, but his workload and the office environment brought him an immense amount of stress.

I never wanted to dread Mondays, no matter what I did to earn money. Thanks to music, I knew there was more to life than a job that had you living for the weekends. Music had been an outlet for me, keeping me hopeful and positive. Now that I had retired from DJing and was back in an office job, I wasn't sure what to do.

I was trying to figure out who the hell I was now, without music and DJing. Being back in a cubicle gave me a steady paycheque, but I needed to find a new channel for my creative energy while I reinvented myself.

Meditation, Ashtanga yoga, biking, and reading things that fuelled my soul had helped me climb my way out of depression. I was journalling regularly and had a wall covered in sticky notes with ideas for a possible book.

Given the focus on writing, a blog seemed like the perfect creative outlet. I was finding joy, meaning, and purpose after coming out of the darkest period in my life. I wanted to share what I was learning and hopefully help others too.

It's out of this intention that my Celebrate Mondays blog was born.

Some of the posts included:

- "It's Totally OK to Feel Like Shit Sometimes"
- A video of me telling the "Without A Paddle Story"
- "Why You Suck At Accomplishing Your Goals"

I published a whopping seven blog posts before it fizzled out. Why did I fail with it?

1. I had no clarity of who my audience was. I didn't know who I was specifically speaking to.
2. I didn't have a writing habit in place to write regularly regardless of how I was feeling. (Inspiration truly is for amateurs.)
3. Deep down, I didn't believe I could do it. I struggled to believe that I could be a writer.

It took some more fumbling around in the years to come, but eventually I realized that if I wanted to create a life where I got to use my experiences to help others, there was more than my belief about not being a writer that would have to change.

27

No You Didn't

At my new job, my direct boss, Shannon, was an incredible woman. She was resilient, determined, resourceful, and supportive. While I loved working with her, the rotating door of people she had reported to since I'd been there included:

- Someone who struggled getting into the office before 11 a.m. and who spent their days shopping online.
- An individual who told the entire team "I have more experience than all of you combined" on their first day before proceeding to show up to work a total of seven times in a four-month span, until she got canned.

- A man based in Arizona who believed that all Canadians lived in igloos.

"I just can't believe that people in Canada ever go to a beach. Isn't it just covered in snow up there?" That was his response when I asked him why he was laughing.

He was the senior leader, based in another country, and had never been to Canada. He was also our fourth new division head in the last half year. He was laughing because when he asked what my plans were for my time off the following week, I shared that I'd likely be going to the beach.

I had been promoted twice in a year and was now in a manager role. I was leading a team of eight people who worked in various cities in two different countries. As the most senior French-speaking person on the team, I was also the lead for our Montéal-based accounts. It might sound fancy, but the pay was terrible for the amount of work and responsibility I had.

"We're happy to offer you this new position but can only give you a $5000 raise," they said when giving me my last promotion.

I'd gotten the same line with a previous promotion. It wasn't Shannon's fault. Human Resources had strict rules around limiting the percentage of an off-cycle raise. Combine that with our division not being particularly profitable and the lack of a reliable leader above her to support any request Shannon might make, there wasn't much she could do.

With my small increases I was no longer losing money every month. My take-home pay was finally enough to cover my living expenses of being a single parent with two young kids living in Toronto. For that, I was grateful.

When doing research on what my salary should be as a manager in my industry, it showed that I was being underpaid by about $20,000 a year. I was aware of this when I accepted the new title. I'd taken the role for the experience and the learning. I knew that if I wouldn't eventually get the pay raise here, I could take the experience and get it somewhere else.

As the months wore on, the lack of senior leadership support fuelled an uncertainty for the future of our department. Shannon was doing everything she could to keep us afloat but we had no one doing business development for us. She was now doing sales, overseeing operations, and still helping with delivery. All this while navigating the political minefield of bullshit above her and managing her own personal stress on the homefront.

Shannon did her best to shield me from it all but she was clearly struggling. The constant critical questioning from senior leaders about our lackluster revenue made it seem like our department could be eliminated at any time. I wasn't enjoying the work either. Other than the strain from juggling the demands of multiple accounts, the personalities involved, and the varied tasks that needed to get done, I wasn't being challenged. I wasn't using my creativity.

Although it doesn't excuse my behaviour, that's likely why I bluntly answered "No you didn't" to a request Shannon insisted she had made.

It was my short and snappy email response to her regarding something she said that she had asked me to do. My reply was rude, out of character, and it upset her. It was clear that the uncertainty and stress was starting to get to me. I was becoming a miserable prick.

It was a turning point. I decided I needed to take action and make a change. Once I made up my mind that I would absolutely find something better, I knew that a shift in the way I was feeling was required. There was no way I could attract, let alone connect with a new exciting opportunity from a place of feeling stressed and unhappy. It simply wouldn't line up.

I started looking for things to be positive about. I deliberately got myself in the habit of feeling joyful on a daily basis, regardless of what went down at work or the current balance of my bank account. I was intentionally finding things to be grateful for, no matter how small.

As I worked on getting myself to routinely feel thankful, I knew what else I had to do. I made the list.

My new role would:

- Be at a growing organization with financial stability
- Allow me to use my creativity
- Have a supportive environment where I could learn
- Be within walking distance from my place (I currently had a seven-minute walk to work)
- Give me a $20,000 raise

I reviewed my list frequently and created the belief that I was destined to find a new, exciting role.

While I was regularly looking at openings online, nothing caught my eye for several weeks.

Then one morning I woke up to a notification that my ex-wife, Monika, had tagged me in a comment on Facebook. Our mutual friend PJ was posting about an opening at the tech company he worked at.

I had seen his post earlier but didn't click through to the job description. Something about the way he had described the role didn't sound appealing. Was I ever wrong. Once I started reading the details, I instantly got excited. This was it. It was a manager position focused on leading employee engagement and fostering company culture. It was a tech-based marketing agency. The job posting was written in a creative way and the company was growing. Thank God Monika had seen it and tagged me on it. I would've missed the chance to learn more about it.

I was asked to an interview and when I arrived, I noticed that the office and staff matched the creativity and energy I had sensed from the role description. There was a Lego wall, the reception desk looked like a spaceship, and my interviews were more like engaging discussions with peers than the interrogations other organizations used in their hiring processes.

The interviews went on over several weeks, and I met a dozen different people over multiple visits. They were being highly selective and intentional with the role. Every time I came into the office I felt confident that I was going to get the job. It wasn't a cocky feeling but it was unwavering.

In the later stages of the interview process I met with Donna, a senior leader who oversaw a large division of the company. We had made an instant connection and she was a master at making others feel comfortable in her presence. It's a stellar approach as an interviewer as it allows you to cut through the performative facade that tends to come with hiring.

I got too comfortable, though.

"You seem extremely calm. Are you sure that you can keep up with the high energy of this team?" Her question was seemingly innocent but I might as well have stepped on a land mine.

"This calmness you see is intentional," I replied. "I've created it from changing my lifestyle and meditating daily. I haven't always been this chill. There's a viral video of me losing my shit on someone."

Oops. I'll take things you should never share in an interview for $500, Alex.

My answer surprised her. She didn't know what to say. I knew I had messed up and her change in body language and tone confirmed it. I managed to instill some energy back into the conversation before we wrapped up, but it didn't end well. I had screwed up.

I didn't sleep at all that night. I was so certain that this was the role I was supposed to get but I was now also equally sure that I had completely bungled it and killed my chances.

What could I do? I started drafting an apology email to send to her but it was getting wordy and it didn't feel like enough. I had massively messed up. I needed an equally big remedy. I needed to be bolder.

My hand shook as I picked up the phone. My throat was dry and my heart was racing. I walked through it in my head. Calling her might not change the outcome but not taking action and avoiding this call guaranteed that I'd lose the opportunity and remain stuck in my current job.

I called the main office number and asked reception to put me through to her. To my surprise she picked up.

"Hi Donna, it's Robb. You interviewed me yesterday for the Manager of People Engagement role. I want to apologize as I royally screwed up in our interview. I mishandled your question when you asked me about being too calm. Not only did my answer not address your question, but also what I shared would definitely make you hesitant to move me forward."

She paused before responding.

"Thank you. I appreciate that. Your answer did catch me off guard and it gave me pause, but I have to say that I'm thoroughly impressed by you right now for making this phone call. It's a hard thing to do. I've never had anyone follow up after an interview like this. I haven't given my feedback on our conversation yet. You calling me will greatly impact what I say."

I was moved forward to the final round: meeting the CEO. It felt like the entire thing was a fun game and now I was facing the final boss.

I met the CEO, Ryan, at 7:30 p.m. in his office. "I heard lots of great things about you," he said. It was nice to hear, but I also knew his opening statement was intentionally checking to see if I had an ego.

Like all my other meetings up to this point, it was much more conversational in tone. We talked about business and psychology. We shared some of our favourite books and why we enjoyed them. He asked for my feedback about the interview process. I'm sure partially out of curiosity, but also to see if I would give it to him straight or blow smoke up his ass. Things went incredibly well. As I left, he gave me a copy of his book.

Two days later, I got the call: I got the job.

My commute to work went from being a seven-minute walk to just five. I got a $23,000 raise, and my creative background was embraced. The fact that I used to be a DJ and music producer was seen as a welcome bonus here.

I had proven to myself again that when I set a clear intention, create internal belief, and align my energy and emotions, I can be the intentional creator of my life. This time around pushed me to take action even when it was incredibly uncomfortable because I had royally fucked up. It showed me that **success is not about trying to avoid failures, missteps, and face plants at all cost. It's about seeing them as an integral part of the journey of learning and growth.**

28

Eulogy

I was settling into my new job. I was starting to pay down my debt, and the kids and I were making memories in our cozy apartment. These were all things I was deeply grateful for as I sat in a coffee shop near my place on a quiet Saturday morning doing some writing and reflecting.

It was the weekend after Easter and the kids and I had visited my family for the holiday. It got me thinking about relationships. In particular, the ones I had with my parents and my brother.

My brother is almost six years younger than me. That meant that we struggled to connect growing up. We were simply in different worlds. While I was discovering parties, dating, and dancing, he was still playing with action figures. By the time he and I were starting to be able to relate, I moved out.

I can't say that I have many memories of us feeling like a family unit growing up. My dad wasn't around much, and my mom didn't like leaving the house. That meant that we rarely did anything with the four of us together and my mom, my brother and I often ate dinner without dad.

That last weekend had been different. We had eaten Easter dinner together and we actually felt like a family. We laughed, shared stories, and enjoyed each other's company.

I smiled at the memory and looked down. There was a newspaper on the coffee shop's wooden table left behind by a previous customer, and an article caught my eye. It was about why the eulogy that Justin Trudeau gave at his father's funeral 13 years earlier had been so impactful.

It was enough to make me look up the speech online and watch a clip. Before I knew it, tears were rolling down my cheeks. It was a beautiful love letter from a son to his father. Given that he delivered it in both English and French, it spoke to me personally.

Hearing it made me realize that some day, I was going to give a eulogy at my father's funeral. Surrounded by strangers enjoying warm drinks and with tears in my eyes, I started taking notes.

What would be all the things I would want to say? What would I want people to know about my father? Why did I love him? Why did I appreciate him? Why was I proud to be his son? Both the words and the tears flowed with ease.

My relationship with my pops hasn't always been easy. There was a period in my youth where I would've been quick to say that I hated him.

He'd been softening up with age and he truly embraced becoming a grandfather. He loved his grandkids and expressed it openly. It had given us a major breakthrough in our relationship a few years earlier, when we were visiting my parents' house and my dad volunteered to change Sébastien's diaper. I stood beside him as he laughed and tickled Sébastien while giving his bottom a wipe. Once he was done cleaning him up, my dad looked at me with watery eyes and said, "I think I've changed more of Sophie and Sébastien's diapers than I ever did of yours and Anthony's. I feel like they're giving me a second chance to right the wrongs I made as a father."

He wasn't one to communicate much emotion so it caught me off guard. As I held Sébastien in one arm, I hugged my dad and thanked him.

I can't say that I had verbalized much love to my father over the years either and a lot poured out of me in the coffee shop that day. When I was done writing all the things I would want to say at his funeral, it hit me. How sad would it be if I waited until he was dead to share this? Why wouldn't I tell him now while he was still alive instead of saving it for a remembrance speech after his passing?

So I put it all in an email. I laid it all out. I let him know just how much I loved and appreciated him.

I thanked him for:

- Instilling honesty in me as a value above all else.
- The big sacrifices he made with his military career when the family needed it most. We came back from England six months earlier than planned because of how our family was struggling overseas. My dad put through a "compassionate posting exemption" request

to make it happen. Because of it, instead of the guaranteed promotion he was supposed to get upon his return to Canada, he was blackballed and never promoted again.

- Doing whatever it took to be able to provide for us, even if it meant driving a cab part-time or working construction.
- Breaking the abuse cycle and not following in his father's footsteps and beating us as kids like he and his siblings had experienced.
- How supportive he'd been of my ambitions. He hadn't always understood what I did or why I was doing it, but if it was what I wanted to do and it made me happy, he supported me in any way he could.
- Helping me out when I was down and in my darkest place. While I couldn't talk to him about the emotions I was struggling with, he lent me the money I needed to pay my first and last month's rent when Monika and I separated.
- Leading by example and showing me that the only way to do a job is with dedication and hard work.
- Being the best grandfather Sophie and

> Sébastien could ever ask for and for his influence on how they were turning out to be incredibly happy, smart, inquisitive, and loving people.

While it was easy to write, I hesitated in sending it. How would he react? Was this going to be too much? What if he simply didn't respond?

I closed my laptop and left the coffee shop without sending it. As I walked home I thought about how there was no point in having written this all out if I wasn't going to share it. As soon as I got home, before I even took off my coat, I opened my laptop and hit send.

It took my dad three long weeks to write back. It was worth the wait. Raw, emotional, and full of gratitude, it's easily the most beautiful message I've ever received from my father.

I'm so grateful that I finally expressed my feelings to my pops. When I was younger it was easy to blame him for the things he did wrong. As I've gotten older I realized that he did the best he could with what he had. If I'm going to blame him for the bad, I have to also credit him for the good. You can't separate the two. There's no way I'd have my drive, my fiery independence, and my rebellious nature if it weren't for him.

I love my father dearly and never miss a chance to say it to him now. I've heard him say I love you more to me in the last 10 years than I had the previous 30 years combined.

There's an amazing realm of possibilities once you let go of anger and resentment. **Don't wait until they're dead. Don't wait until the eulogy.**

Me, pops, and my brother Anthony in Montréal in 2021

29
You Can't Do That

It was December 21st, the shortest day of the year in the northern hemisphere and the season when people are planning their New Year's resolutions. A friend invited me to join them at a winter solstice celebration and we milled through a street parade that felt more like a carnival. Surrounded by fire breathers and musicians, I admired an oversized papier-mâché snow owl that stood more than 20 feet tall on the end of thick bamboo sticks. It required a team of people to hold it up. The owl was frosty blue and white with bright yellow eyes. I wondered how many hours had they spent making it?

As the procession came to an end, hundreds of us gathered in a circle to watch a big art structure burn.

It felt ceremonial. It also reminded me of Burning Man and how I hoped to return to the desert event one day.

It was a surprisingly mild December night, which meant it was raining instead of snowing. We made our way indoors to warm up and dry off. It was a dimly lit venue with a narrow bar area near the entrance and an open space in the back where people were dancing to funk music. We stayed near the front where people were doing their best to engage in some sort of conversation over the music. Everyone was holding a drink in their hands and I felt a familiar subconscious pressure building in me.

I didn't want to drink. Earlier in the week I had been bedridden with an intense flu and a fever so high I had hallucinations. In one of the dreams, I could fold my body in half like Play-Doh. In another, I had a nightmare that if I didn't get all the wrinkles out of my bedsheets my flu would never end, which felt like an impossible task in my weakened state, dripping in sweat as I was.

I was feeling better now. Kinda. But maybe only a six out of ten. Even though I knew deep down that I definitely didn't want to be drinking, I caved. Within minutes of walking in I found myself at the bar ordering my go-to: Jäger on the rocks. My internal voice didn't waste any time spewing self-judgement. "Really? You're *that* weak, Robb?"

"You alright?" my friend asked. She could tell that something was off. I'd gone silent in an internal guilt spiral over the drink I was now holding in my hands.

"I'm not drinking all of next year," I said. The words came out of my mouth before I even had a chance to think about them.

I got a blank, surprised stare in return.

"I mean it, I'm not drinking all of next year," I said.

"You can't do that."

It was the best response I could've gotten. A challenge.

Being told I can't do something is one of my strongest motivators. The rebel in me loves proving others wrong when they cast doubt about what I can and can't do.

I had done short dry spells before. Typically after the hangover and shame of an alcohol-fuelled night was too much to bear. But the longest I had ever gone was two months. It never lasted. I was too good at telling myself legitimate-sounding reasons to give booze another chance.

"I'll start drinking again but keep it to a couple of drinks when I do" and "This truly is a special event that deserves celebrating" were some of my staples. All lies.

I put my glass down on the bar without finishing my drink. Now that I had made my decision, I no longer felt the need to keep drinking. Would I be able to go an entire year without alcohol? It's not something I'd done since the first time I got drunk in Grade 7. That was 24 years ago.

30

Starts With A Kiss

"You weren't supposed to be like this."

It's the last thing I said as we were parting ways at the end of our first date.

Melissa and I had met on a dating site. Her profile outlined that she was looking for adventure, not a life partner. I was coming out of another relationship and not ready for anything serious, either.

While hilarious and engaging, our text exchanges had been filled with flirting, not thoughtful questions that would help us assess our compatibility as long-term partners.

"I'll meet you at 6 p.m. I'm not going to say a word when I walk up. I'm going to grab you and kiss you. Our date starts with a kiss," I wrote to her, as we planned our first meetup.

That evening, she was standing alone at our meeting spot when I arrived. She had black hair, a black jacket and a look of nervous excitement in her eyes. Her shy smile as I walked up made me 100% certain that I was about to smooch the right woman. Placing one hand behind her head and the other behind her lower back, I leaned in for a kiss without saying a thing. She was shorter than I'd expected. I literally picked her off her feet.

As I pulled away from our embrace, we locked eyes and smiled.

"Hi," I said.

"Hi," she replied.

We made our way to a restaurant located in an old house nearby. With exposed brick, furniture made from unfinished wood, and candles in every corner, it was warm and cozy.

The restaurant wasn't busy. Between the lack of other patrons and our complete focus on each other, it felt like we were the only ones there. We talked about everything from what might have happened if she was late for our meetup and I had tried to kiss a random stranger, to how much business would the restaurant need to do on weekends to make up for how slow it was on this Tuesday, and what was the etiquette, since I was an idiot and had ordered a dish full of garlic on a first date—should she eat some of my meal? (She did.)

Our second makeout session went down before leaving the restaurant. I pounced on her as she was walking out of the washroom and threw her against the wall. She was surprised and enthusiastic. It was a heated exchange.

She was kind, genuine, warm hearted, and hilarious. She was beautiful and extra attractive when she laughed. She was witty. She could talk business and laugh about my screwups without missing a beat. I liked her. A lot.

"You weren't supposed to be like this" meant I wasn't supposed to like her this much.

31
Second Date

I'd been at my new job for a few months. The accompanying raise didn't mean I had money to burn, but it meant I no longer needed to worry about my debit card getting declined at the grocery store checkout. I was building a buffer and it gave me hope.

The morning after my birthday, I found myself delaying going to work and scrolling on Facebook. It wasn't that I was tired or hungover—quite the opposite. The night before had been full of reflection, as my birthdays tended to be. I was feeling grateful and craving adventure.

I'd initially logged on to Facebook to acknowledge and thank all the people wishing me a happy birthday. Instead of getting ready to go to the office once I was done, I risked being late and followed an internal nudge to scroll a bit longer.

"I've got WestJet flight passes that expire on Monday. You just have to pay the taxes. Anyone want them?"

The post leapt off the screen of my white 13-inch MacBook. I couldn't believe it. The person who had posted it was Erin, a friend I'd met through music.

I had goosebumps as I typed a note.

"Hi! Any chance you have passes left? I'd love to skip out somewhere sunny this weekend. It was my birthday yesterday," I wrote to her. I mentioned my birthday hoping it might give me an edge if she received multiple messages.

"If you can use them this weekend, you can have them," she wrote back. "They need to be used by Monday. Let me know where you're hoping to go and I'll check seat availability since you'd be flying standby."

I looked up WestJet's route map. They flew to some Caribbean destinations, but the flights weren't as frequent. I also wanted to spend the least amount of time in the air given this was going to be a short trip.

Then I saw it—Miami! It was perfect. It was just a three-hour jaunt and they had regular flights so it would be easier getting a seat. Plus, WestJet also flew to Fort Lauderdale, which is only 35 minutes from Miami. That would give me a second airport option to reduce my chances of getting stuck in southern Florida.

I knew my way around Miami. I'd been there a bunch of times for the annual music conference and to DJ at Ultra Music Festival. The South Beach neighbourhood was a gem with its beautiful beaches, stellar restaurants, and romantic art deco buildings.

My destination was set, but who would I bring?

"Want to go to Miami this weekend?" I texted Melissa on my way to grab lunch.

"Are you serious?!" Melissa wrote back almost instantly.

It was a valid question. I was casually asking her to fly to another country with me that weekend and it was already lunchtime on Thursday. Not to mention that we'd only gone on our first date two days prior.

"I'm dead serious. I've got flight passes. We'd fly out early Saturday morning and come back late Sunday. You won't have to take any time off work."

There was a pause before her next message.

"You're going to turn my life upside down!"

That wasn't the intention, but I understood why she was feeling that way.

"What if you murder me and leave my body in Florida?" she asked.

She was joking, but there's a dash of truth in every joke. I *was* proposing that she fly to a city 2400 kilometres away with someone she barely knew for a second date.

"I'll send you pictures of my passport," I replied. "You can give them to your sister and best friend."

Finally Melissa agreed. I gave Erin our information and she registered us to fly standby on a 7:45 a.m. direct flight to Miami. Erin noted that the flight had some open seats but not an overwhelming amount. "You should be OK given that the departure is in less than 36 hours."

As Melissa and I fleshed out our plans, I shared my rule of not checking luggage. I wasn't George

Clooney's character in the movie *Up In the Air*, but I had travelled plenty thanks to music. It meant that I had personal travel rules. The one I was stickiest about was never checking bags. Carry-on only. Having luggage lost or delayed is the easiest way to disrupt a trip. I learned this lesson the hard way 15 years earlier when I had checked luggage that never made its way to my destination.

Melissa expressed concerns about being restricted to a small suitcase. "There's beach attire, casual wear, and I need a dress and different shoes in case we go out for a nice dinner. Plus, I need warmer clothes for our trip home. I can't fit that all in a carry-on."

Thanks mostly to the brevity of the trip, I was able to convince her otherwise. I'd have to work on permanently enrolling her into the carry-on only club if this evolved into a serious relationship.

"We can use my airport driver Gus to take us to the airport," Melissa added.

I couldn't help but wonder, why did she have her own airport driver? How often did she travel? What else did I not know about this woman? We were about to spend an intense 40 hours straight together and we really didn't know much about each other.

It was pitch black out when Gus picked me up on Saturday morning. There was snow on the ground and I could see my breath in the frosty air. I was looking forward to the warm Florida weather. Erin had messaged me late the night before to let me know that while there were still a few seats open on the flight, it was looking tighter. A surprising number of people had purchased last-minute tickets. As we pulled up to the airport, it also dawned on me that the weekend would be a trial of our compatibility as a couple.

Melissa and I made our way to our gate and took a seat. My phone buzzed—it was Erin. The flight was now nearly full and it wasn't looking good as there were some people ahead of us on standby.

We listened as names of other standby passengers were called up. They were getting tickets. Maybe we had a chance? We'd get our answer soon enough, as we watched the plane push back off the gate from the big windows inside the airport.

The disappointment didn't last. Erin was a gate check agent for the airline and was working at the airport that morning. She was determined to get us to our destination. Erin worked her magic and switched our passes to a Fort Lauderdale flight that was leaving an hour later. It was only half full and a breeze getting on.

I'd booked us a room at a cute Art Deco hotel on Ocean Drive thanks to an online deal. We spent two days hanging out on the beach, sharing yummy food, and strolling the streets of South Beach. We admired jellyfish that had washed ashore at sunrise and kissed under the stars on the sand at night. Our conversation threads weaved through sharing childhood memories, our biggest dreams, and the challenges we'd faced with our parents. We dissected the business model of the cute sandwich stand we ate lunch at and schemed what we'd do if we got stuck in Miami. If it sounds like one of those cheesy romantic comedy movies that are centred around long, ongoing conversations, it kind of was. But it didn't feel cheesy. It felt real. It felt hopeful.

I never found out why she had her own airport driver but I did learn so much more about Melissa that weekend. As we cuddled at the gate while waiting for our flight home Sunday night, it occurred to me: If I thought I liked Melissa too much after our first date, I was in over my head after our second.

32

How Things Feel

A month into dating, Melissa got another offer to travel. This time a destination wedding in Mexico. She would be going away for a week.

Things hadn't slowed down after we got back from Miami. The intimacy created from travelling together had only sped things up. By any metric, we were in a serious relationship.

We were talking daily, discussing the future, and went one eight-day stretch where we saw each other every single day. It was intense but exciting.

The timing of her trip worked well. I was busy at work and had plenty to do at home to get the kids and I settled into our new place. After two years of living in a tiny one-bedroom apartment, I was finally able to move us into a bigger spot. The kids had their own room and I no longer had to sleep on the couch.

Melissa and I didn't talk much the week she was away. Things went from being full-on to a hard stop overnight. After a whirlwind month together, the pause gave me a chance to think. Was this what I wanted? Was I ready for a relationship? I wasn't sure that I was.

I felt my chest tighten as I picked up the phone. I was nervous. I knew what I needed to say. I didn't want to hurt Melisssa but I knew what had to be done.

"I've had a lot of time to reflect and I want to put things on hold," I told her. "I know I egged this on, but I'm not ready for a relationship right now."

Melissa was back from her trip and I was breaking up with her.

There was a pause before she responded. Melissa was surprised, upset, and hurt. I had been hot, hot, hot, and now I was suddenly cold. Not wanting to believe it really was the end, she asked for us to have another date.

"Let's go out one more time to see how things feel," she said.

It was a fair request. The connection between us in person was strong.

I agreed. I was an asshole for suddenly wanting to cut things off after being so intense. It was the least I could do. She had happily come along for the ride, but she had definitely followed my lead. Maybe I was making a rash decision in wanting to end it?

We made plans to go see a movie together and then hang out afterwards. I can't say that the movie choice determined the outcome, but in retrospect it's easy to see how the movie influenced where we landed.

If you haven't seen *The Imitation Game*, I'm about to spoil it for you. It's based on the life of brilliant British mathematician Alan Turing, who led the team responsible for decoding the German Enigma machine. This feat allowed the Allies to understand all of Germany's secret military communication without the Nazis knowing. The movie was intense but historians estimate this breakthrough shortened the war by two years and helped save 14 million lives.

The movie doesn't have a happy ending, though—quite the opposite. Alan Turing's life had a miserable and cruel ending. He was arrested and given a chemical castration to "cure" him of being a homosexual, and after a year of government-mandated hormonal therapy, he committed suicide.

As the lights came on in the theatre, Melissa and I looked at each other in stunned silence. It was sad and heartbreaking. Not much was said as we left the theatre or on our subway ride home afterwards. I let her know that I hadn't changed my mind. We were done, for now.

33
Nuberto

After prioritizing my mental and physical health for several years, my creative urge to make music started coming back. I had walked away from music so thoroughly before when things had gotten bad in my life, that it didn't feel OK to start releasing music as Robb G again.

If I was going to make music, it would need to be under a new name and have a deeper purpose. I bought a new laptop and flew to San Francisco to spend the weekend with my friend Dylan. We caught up while he helped me get my new computer set up with the newest software and synths to begin making music.

Instead of simply coming up with a new alias, I created an inspirational project incognito called Nuberto. The video announcing the project launch laid out 50 goals with the aim of achieving them all in two years. The listed objectives got increasingly more difficult as they progressed. I launched the project anonymously on Facebook and Instagram and invited people to follow along.

This was the project's description:

"A music project, a dream, and an experiment. I'm doing this to show what's possible when we have the courage to set outrageous goals and work towards them."

Here were the 50 Goals:

1. Get 50 shares on a post
2. Have a release on Mad Decent
3. Get 50,000 views or plays on a video or song
4. Play at The Exchange (L.A.)
5. Play at The Hoxton (Toronto)
6. Play at Webster Hall (N.Y.)
7. Get 250,000 views or plays on a video or song
8. Have a release on Owsla
9. Have a top 10 song in a Beatport genre chart

10. Sign to a management company with an established roster
11. Sign with a big agency (either AM Only, WME , or CAA)
12. Play an early slot on a festival main stage
13. Get photographed by Maria Supermaniak
14. Work with A-Trak on a project
15. Get scratch lessons from Skratch Bastid
16. Get 500,000 views or plays on a video or song
17. Have a song included on the fresh EDM Spotify list
18. Collab with Andrew Huang on a project
19. Have a song played on BBC Radio 1
20. Have a #1 song in a Beatport genre chart
21. Play at Shambhala Festival (B.C.)
22. Get mix down tips from Wolfgang Gartner
23. Get photographed at a gig by Rukes
24. Get 1 million views or plays on a video or song
25. Secret Goal
26. Get 1000 shares on a post

27. Have a guest set on SiriusXM
28. Play at Ultra Music Festival (Miami)
29. Appear on the #AskGaryVee Show
30. Play at Electric Daisy Carnival (Nevada or N.Y.)
31. Play at Ushuaïa (Ibiza)
32. Play at Octagon (Korea)
33. Have a release on Spinnin'
34. Have a guest set on BBC Radio 1
35. Play at Surrender (Las Vegas)
36. Play at Tomorrowland (Belgium)
37. Work with HI-LO on a project
38. Journée dans le studio avec DJ Snake
39. Play at Stereosonic Festival (Australia)
40. Play at Glastonbury (U.K.)
41. Pay it forward: Get an up-and-comer a dream opening slot
42. Remix either Fatboy Slim or Moby
43. Get 5 million views or plays on a video or song
44. Have a #1 overall song on Beatport

45. Get interviewed by Tim Ferriss
46. Have lunch with Jim Carrey
47. Play at Coachella (California)
48. Have a top 10 on the iTunes dance chart
49. Remix Drake
50. Sign a book deal about the project

The launch video got 456 likes and 200 shares on Facebook. It wasn't long before my new music was getting radio plays and I was receiving messages from people saying that I was inspiring them. I was having fun, making music, and uplifting others.

The challenge was that when I created the list of goals, I focused too much on making sure they would be inspiring to others. While a couple of them would still be incredible to this day, such as getting interviewed by Tim Ferriss or having lunch with Jim Carrey, many of them weren't deeply aligned for me personally. I didn't really want to be DJing at all these festivals nor did I feel motivated to sign music to the record labels I listed. It's what I thought others would find exciting. This was a fatal flaw.

The 50 objectives were essentially a "do these things and you're a mega Electronic Dance Music

(EDM) superstar" list. That's not who I wanted to be. This meant that when I hit inevitable challenges, like you do with every project, I gave up— my heart just wasn't into it. I did want to inspire others and show them they could achieve things far beyond what they believed, but I had no interest in being an EDM superstar.

Nuberto was added to the pile of projects I started that failed. I clearly felt a calling for helping and inspiring others. I just needed to find a more authentic way of doing it.

34
Dancing in Seoul

I was on vacation in Seoul with the girl I was dating and it was our last night in the city. We were wandering the Hongdae neighbourhood when we stumbled across a dance circle. Close to the university, this part of town is full of bars and nightclubs, and packed with thousands of 20-somethings milling about on the streets on any night of the week. It's here, down a side street, in a dimly lit playground, where I hesitated.

"This isn't a show—we need your participation to keep going," the voice over the loudspeaker said.

Bass music was blasting, and the person with the mic was looking for members of the audience to participate and dance.

I knew the drill. I'd been jumping into dance circles to bust a move since grade school. The first memory I have of boogying for a crowd was dancing on a picnic table to Michael Jackson for the enjoyment of drunk neighbours when I was six. There are few things I love more than moving my body to music, and I was no stranger to doing it in front of others.

My big blue eyes stood out everywhere we'd been that week. At six foot three, I was a giant in local crowds and had to duck to get through the Korean subway doors. The further we ventured from the city centre, the more people stared. Most didn't even pretend not to look.

We had stopped to watch because I told my partner that I wanted to dance. She stood and waited for me to step in. I had been cool with being the centre of attention all week. But now I was frozen with fear.

"I'll wait for the next song," I said to my girlfriend. But the next song came and went.

"I'll go after the next person," I said then. But the next dancer came and went.

The excuses kept coming and I wasn't moving. My heart was screaming to dance. But I was stalling.

What if I messed up? What if I made a fool of myself?

When it seemed like no one else was going to, I finally took a step forward. At that same moment, a man in a suit was called out by the guy with the mic. The dance crew knew him, called him by name, and asked the crowd to applaud for "one of the best dancers in Seoul."

He was hesitant too. He was in a dress shirt and carrying a leather work bag. He seemed tired and it looked like he was making his way home from the office. He shook his head to indicate that he wasn't interested. They continued egging him on.

When he realized that they weren't going to stop, he gave a shrug. He loosened his tie and started to manoeuvre his body to the beats. He was incredible. His movements easily shifted from jagged chest stutters to flowing arm movements. All of it was perfectly in sync with the sounds of the music.

I was in awe. There was no way I could follow him. I'd go after someone else. But no one else went. They called for participation. No one moved.

"Last chance."

I stalled. The moment passed and the organizers began to pack things up. My girlfriend looked confused and disappointed.

"What happened? Why didn't you dance?" she asked.

"I don't know" is all I could muster. I had let fear dictate my actions and stop me from doing something that I absolutely loved. Now I felt embarrassed because of it.

They say it's not what you do that you'll regret the most, it's what you don't do. Not dancing that night in Seoul would haunt me until I found a way to fix things in Paris two years later.

35
People Mistakes

I needed a break. Things hadn't been going well in the dating department and work was increasingly being dominated by politics and posturing that I wasn't interested in.

I booked a trip to visit a friend, Christine, in Todos Santos, a sleepy surf town with dreamy private beaches on the Baja California Peninsula of Mexico. Christine had upended her life, sold her house, and moved to Mexico with a friend of hers to start fresh. She had gone completely against the grain and it was inspiring.

We spent the week having healthy eats, reading, writing, doing yoga, and sitting on the beach watching whales spout water in the distance. It was exactly what I needed. The day before I was heading home, I briefly checked my work email. I got quiet after and my friend noticed.

"What's on your mind?"

"Work. I just checked my inbox."

"What does the company do again?"

"Marketing."

"Oh." She seemed surprised.

"What kind of products?"

"Pharmaceuticals. Many of the world's biggest pharma companies are our clients."

She paused before saying the part that stung.

"I don't know what to say other than that's surprising. It doesn't seem to line up with your values."

Huh. I had gotten so wrapped up in the teaching, training, and the coaching aspects of my job that I loved so much that I had kind of forgotten what the company actually did and lost sight of how that was perceived outside of my work bubble.

My life revolved around work. I had never been around so many brilliant, creative, and entrepreneurial-minded people before. The intense hours, pressure to always be at your best, and constantly reinforced messages about how "different" and "special" the company culture was created an environment where deep bonds were forged with fellow co-workers.

We spent so much time together sharing wild and unique experiences, we figured outsiders simply didn't "get it." The official onboarding booklet waiting for me on my desk on my first day had the word "fuck" in it, twice. We had work events where Margaret Atwood and David Cronenberg were speakers. An annual all-employee lakeside sleepover camp in the woods with an open bar. And our office had a squash court because the CEO was really into squash at the time it was built.

My life was so intertwined with work that I even broke the cardinal rule and dated someone from the office for a while. A friend outside the company had pointed out that my job gave me what many get in college or university: a group of bright, like-minded people to share ideas and party with. That part was a blast.

But I had got too caught up in fitting in and too

wrapped up in the story behind the place. If there was one thing the organization was good at marketing, it was selling how great of a place it was to work at—both to the external world and to its own employees. Open bar events with celebrity guests, lavish employee gifts such as Apple Watches, and high-production promotional videos with YouTube stars—millions of dollars were spent reinforcing the message.

I hadn't only bought into the story, I was also one of its chief peddlers. Every Monday, I had a new cohort of hires that I was indoctrinating in "how awesome this place is" as part of a week-long onboarding program that I had created. I was so deep in it that I couldn't see it for myself. I needed the outside perspective. Christine's observation after a reflective week in Mexico surrounded by natural beauty was snapping me out of it.

I landed in Toronto on a Sunday night and was back in the office the next day. I felt out of sorts and out of place. Over lunch, I sat looking up at the clouds as if the answers I needed were going to be in the sky.

"I wish there was a way for me to get some more paid time off so I could figure out what I'm going to do next" is what I said to myself.

There was no way that could happen. My work was backed up from just taking a week off, and we had a big cohort of new hires starting the following Monday.

I made my way back to the office as I had a one on one with my manager, Emma. I knocked on the door.

"Come in," she said. The head of finance was sitting there with her.

"Oh, I can come back later," I said.

"Phil is joining us. Have a seat," Emma said.

As I closed the door behind me and sat down, I sensed something was off. Phil, who I normally laughed and joked with, was avoiding eye contact.

"Today is your last day," Emma said.

My mind raced as I tried to process what she said. As I sat quietly in disbelief with my mouth open, Emma slid the envelope with the details across the table to me. I opened it, hoping to find answers that would help me make sense of what was happening.

"Unfortunately we feel that the fit is simply no longer there" was the reason listed on my termination letter. They didn't offer any additional explanation and they were giving me the bare minimum legal notice, too. A few weeks of severance.

I was in complete shock.

"Do you want to gather your own stuff and clean out your desk?" Emma asked.

"That's a nightmare!" I replied.

The thought of doing a drawn-out walk of shame by packing up my own desk sounded like brutal punishment.

Phil escorted me out. As we were standing and waiting for the elevator, I almost asked "Does that mean I'm out for good and I can't reapply for other jobs here in the future?" I felt so desperate. I had been voted off the island.

I had onboarded more than 250 new employees here over the last year, worked evenings and weekends for months on end when our team was short staffed, and had personally taken two different employees who had injured themselves at work events to the emergency room. This is how it was ending? This is how they were treating me?

Walking home, my mind was a mess. What was I going to say to the kids? How long could I afford the apartment without a job? Would I lose joint custody of Sophie and Sébastien if I lost the apartment? Fuck.

I cried so much over the following days and weeks.

Deep down I knew this change was ultimately for the better, but it was also extremely painful. Being fired delivers a big blow to your confidence. I replayed conversations and often found myself thinking through what I could have done differently. How could I have avoided this?

The outpouring of support from my co-workers was immense. I got DMs, texts, and emails from dozens of people saying how much I was appreciated, how sorry they were for what happened, and offers to help. It wouldn't pay my bills and didn't stop the tears, but it was nice to know I was appreciated.

I made arrangements with Phil to meet up with someone on his team in the evening the following week to get my stuff. I showed up at the office at 7 p.m. and was surprised to find Phil there himself. He wanted to talk. He apologized for how things were handled. It felt sincere. He said my departure had created an internal stir. He was sorry for how things went down and reinforced that it should've been done differently.

He let me know that Thomas, the co-founder and COO, wanted to meet up with me for lunch. He wanted to apologize in person for how things were handled. It was surprising but it felt nice.

I coordinated with Thomas' assistant to schedule the lunch meeting. After some back and forth, we settled on a date a couple of weeks out so that Ryan, the CEO and other co-founder, could join us. He also wanted to see me face to face.

We were meeting at a popular small sushi joint near the office that was known to get packed over lunch. On the day of the meeting, I went to the restaurant early. I wanted to choose our table. I selected a spot near the entrance where my back would be comfortably against the wall and theirs would be exposed to the highest traffic area in the restaurant. They had asked for the meeting and my confidence had taken a huge blow from all of this. You better believe that I made sure the environment of our meeting favoured me.

Thomas got there first. He thanked me for meeting with them as he sat down. I didn't say much. Ryan arrived a few minutes later and opened by saying that they wanted to meet to apologize in person. A lengthy apology followed.

I sat quietly and listened. There were natural pauses where I could have easily relieved the tension by saying "Thank you" or "I appreciate it." But I didn't. I knew that if I bit my tongue, they'd have to keep talking or it would've been awkward. And they did. It'll likely go down as the single longest apology I'll hear in this lifetime.

Of everything they said, two things stood out above everything else:

1. "This is one of the biggest people mistakes we've ever made."
2. "I don't suppose you'd want to come back?"

There was no going back. It had been almost a month at this point. I was no longer crying every day but I was still grieving. Can you imagine how awkward that would've been? "Yeah, they fired me, but now I'm back after a month off because they realized it was a people mistake."

They offered to extend my pay for as long as I needed. They'd cover me until I found a new gig. They also said I could tell prospective new employers that it was an amicable layoff due to a restructure.

I sincerely thanked Thomas and Ryan. Their

apologies and remorse felt genuine. I was particularly grateful for their offer to support me during the transition. It meant I no longer needed to worry about losing my apartment and joint custody of the kids.

I left feeling relieved and vindicated. I was getting the paid time off to figure out what I was going to do next and find something better aligned to my values. The price to do so was the death of my identity that was deeply embedded in the company and the role I was being set free from. Who was I and who did I want to become now?

36

We'll Break You

Several people had asked the same question that day given that it was New Year's Eve and my self-imposed challenge to not drink for a year was coming to an end.

"Are you going to have a drink at midnight?"

"I don't know" is what I said in response, over and over again. It was an honest answer.

I was at a friend's place with about 20 other people for New Year's Eve. It's the biggest party night of the year. People get dressed up and let loose to usher in the start of a fresh year in the Gregorian calendar. Even those who rarely party go all out on New Year's Eve. Friends of mine in the bar and nightclub industry used to call it "amateur night" because of the behaviour on display.

Doing this year-long challenge had taught me a lot about myself and about the way society treats people who don't drink.

Physical dependencies and addictions aside, there are two aspects of not drinking that can make it challenging.

1. The habits, routines, and associations you have with consuming alcohol.

Drinking is so common and interwoven into our societal norms, that you don't realize it until you're not drinking. Think of all the times and places where drinking is normal, if not expected:

- Birthday parties
- Dinner with friends
- Sporting events
- Patios in the summer
- Work social events
- Weddings
- Pubs, bars, nightclubs

- The entire holiday season
- Any celebration

Beyond outright peer pressure, if your habit is to order a glass of wine whenever you go for dinner with friends, it will feel super odd if you don't. It's the same if you've always had a beer when you go to a sporting event: It will feel really weird going to a game and not having a drink. The two are connected. It's expected by you and the other people you're with.

2. The questions by those who are drinking.

If you decide to take a break from drinking, you can expect to get one of two questions, frequently.

"Why don't you drink?" and "Why aren't you drinking?"

It's as if those who are drinking can't possibly fathom why anyone else would choose not to drink. I knew there would be questions when I opted to not drink for 12 months, but the amount of judgement I received and justification required on my part blew my mind.

Friends, co-workers, and even complete strangers felt that they had both the need and the authority to question and challenge my sobriety. The most surprising incident was having a senior leader declare

"We'll break you and I'll be there when we do" in a job interview.

Doing my booze-free challenge for an entire year gave me lots of practice at answering the barrage of questions. They ranged from harmlessly intended inquiries out of genuine curiosity to outright aggressive interrogation.

I tried and tested various different ways to communicate that I wished to not drink to minimize the follow-up questions and judgement.

Here they are, grouped by the results they produced:

Statements that generated the most follow-up questions: "I quit drinking," "I don't drink," and "I'm taking a break from drinking."

Statements that were hit or miss depending on the context: A simple "No thanks" and "I'm doing a dry (week, month, etc.)."

Statements that generated the least amount of follow-up questions: "I'm driving/I'm the designated driver tonight" and "I used to have a drinking problem/I'm an alcoholic."

Why anyone should have to justify why they're

choosing to not drink seems crazy to me. You have no idea what the other person has been through.

The New Year's Eve countdown was now only 15 minutes away. I was still undecided.

The easy thing would be to have a drink to ring in the new year with everyone. Someone said to me, "You can just have the champagne toast, nothing else." Another friend told me it could be in celebration of me accomplishing my goal.

My intuition, however, was saying, "Why would you throw it away now?"

It had been hard initially: Answering all the questions, changing my own habits and behaviours, and shifting the expectations of those around me, which sometimes required shifting the actual people I had around me. But it was much easier to not drink now. I had created a new identity. I was Robb who was sober and lived booze free. Robb who had more energy, clarity, and focus. Robb who felt better physically, mentally, and spiritually. Robb who had not once woken up in a shame-infused hangover in the last year.

I was proud of myself and I knew that I was better off without alcohol in my life. I had wanted to stop drinking for such a long time and had failed on multiple attempts. I didn't believe I could do it. Now I'd done it for a full year.

It was time for the countdown: 5, 4, 3, 2, 1.....

"Happy New Year!" everyone called out.

I toasted with a glass of plain tonic water. No champagne for me.

As of writing this, it's been almost eight years since I've had a drink. At this point I'd like to tell you that it's a permanent thing. But saying that feels daunting. It feels like unnecessary pressure. Instead, what I can say for certain is, I'm not drinking today.

37

Fake Dates

I can't say that it's true for every couple that spends a weekend in Miami for their second date, but for Melissa and I, it wasn't the winning recipe for a long-term relationship. At least, not initially.

The first time around, things had happened fast. I got in over my head and wasn't ready for something serious.

When Melissa and I first started talking again years later, we went on a series of what we now refer to as fake dates. They were hangouts where we spent hours together, shared meals, went on walks, and got into deep conversations, but there was no hand holding and no kissing.

One time she messaged me to say she was having a bad day. I invited her to join me at Fran's, a 24-hour breakfast diner. She opened up about what was bothering her and I listened while eating a piece of apple pie.

On another occasion, she asked me if I wanted to go to the National Home Show with her. Was I interested in the event? Not at all! The event promised more than 800 vendors showcasing all things home and garden. Not my jam.

But going meant quality time with Melissa and I thoroughly enjoyed hanging out with her. Our talks flowed from brainstorming business opportunities to discussing emotional trauma to sharing dark humour. You never knew where the conversation might go.

I put it in my calendar and met her the morning of the show. We wandered through the venue as if we were walking the streets of Paris. The landmarks were just funnier. There were hot tubs for sale with monthly payment plans, and a plethora of weird appliances—from small items like a banana slicer to an all-in-one Breakfast Station. (Picture a toaster oven with a coffee maker built into its side and an egg and sausage griddle on top. There's a reason why you've never heard of it.)

After grabbing a snack we made ourselves at home in a big, round canopy-covered chair like those you see at fancy beach resorts. We even had our own waterfront view: a hose-powered water fountain.

We talked about the top cities we wanted to travel to and our past relationships while laying side by side. We were lost in conversation and hadn't noticed that the crowd had thinned out until someone with a less-than-cheerful tone informed us that "The show is closed, you have to leave."

As we were walking out, I thought to myself, "I could see myself spending a long time with this woman."

The fake dating went on for months until Melissa invited me to be her date for her friend's wedding.

The drastically different approach to dating the second time around has allowed us to build a rock-solid foundation based on us being there for each other. We see our primary roles as caring for one another, supporting each other's growth, and being a reassuring voice when the other needs it most. We call each other "care buddies." Everything else is secondary.

38

Rich People Are Assholes

Melissa was sitting on the stairs crying. She didn't want to go. I was trying to convince her to join me at a weekend workshop on leadership, connecting with your higher self, and nurturing your inner child. The weekend event promised to "help you uncover your limiting beliefs and become unstoppable."

I had been to one of their teaser events. They leveraged games and team building to open you up to new ways of thinking. The profound shifts previous attendees talked about made it clear that the experience was therapeutic for many.

It was a commitment. The days ran long—from 9 a.m. to midnight, three days in a row. I was eager to go. I devoured new learning about leadership and self-development. I knew I had lots of inner work to do if I wanted to make a leap and start fully living from a place of purpose instead of fear. Melissa was hesitant to attend because she values her privacy and doesn't like talking about personal things with many people, let alone in a room full of strangers.

I was excited at the prospect of Melissa and I doing this together. We could grow together and have it as a shared experience. I was also afraid of going without her. If it gave me a quantum leap like I hoped it would, I didn't want it to create a great divide between us.

As we talked it through, she acknowledged not wanting me to go without her as it would potentially fuel us growing apart. That was the clincher and she agreed to come.

The days were long, fun, emotional, and magical. We left each night both physically and emotionally drained, carrying new understandings about ourselves and the world around us. Tears were shed in the workshop and on our drives home.

It was inspiring to see Melissa there. She faced fears and tried things beyond her regular level of comfort in multiple situations. She was clearly a leader, albeit a quieter, more introverted one. In two different group games, her team won thanks to her strategic thinking and influence.

One of the weekend's most impactful takeaways for me was becoming aware of what I subconsciously believed about rich people: That they are assholes. The realization floored me but it made so much sense.

My parents never had much money. They weren't particularly great with managing the money they did get, either. We never went hungry, but my parents carried debts for years. We lived in the subsidized housing provided to soldiers on military bases because my parents didn't have the savings for a down payment on a house.

The only reason they were able to break the cycle and finally buy their own place when I was in my late 20s was because my dad's job got reclassified. He was given several years of back pay at once after it was deemed he had been underpaid for the role he was performing. He had spent several years being understandably bitter about being shortchanged, but they had actually done him a favour. It forced him to save and he got a lump sum of tens of thousands of dollars in one shot. That's how they got their down payment.

How could I ever let myself get wealthy if I believed deep down that it'd make me an asshole? It would be impossible. When people talk about self-sabotage, this is what it means. You have some deeply held belief, that you might not even be aware of, and it's influencing your choices and behaviour. In my case, a false belief was preventing me from ever hitting a certain level of wealth because I subconsciously believed that having a certain amount of money would make me an asshole. It's absurd.

Now, whenever I see a really high-end car or luxury house, I say to myself "that person provided a lot of value." It may or may not be true, but **if I'm going to tell myself stories about strangers, they might as well be ones that serve me**.

39

Dancing In Paris

When I unplug, when I give my soul room to breathe, when I give myself permission to ignore my inbox, notifications, and social media, my creativity explodes.

That's why I cut the cord for at least a few continuous hours every week and for a full weekend at least once a month. It also means that if a vacation doesn't lead to some big aha and monumental shift in my life, I end up making some memorable creative output. It could be a song, a video, or a whole lot of writing.

On a trip to Paris with Melissa, I got the idea of shooting a video of me dancing at some of the city's memorable landmarks. This decision led to the scariest thing I've done in recent years: dancing in the Louvre.

You're not supposed to dance in public and especially not inside a famous museum where people are quietly admiring some of the most famous works of art in the world. What if people stare? What if security gives me hell? What if we get kicked out of the museum?

I picked my spot and put my headphones in. Melissa gave me the sign that she was ready to film me. But I hesitated. My heart was pounding and people were watching me.

I was filled with hesitation and doubt. It's something we can all relate to. It's that moment before you…

Hit send.

Speak up.

Press post.

Step on the stage.

Start recording a video.

Reach out to a potential client.

We've all been there. Sometimes your inner doubter wins. Sometimes your brave self prevails.

There's a question I ask myself when I'm hesitating in those moments, when doubt is trying to get a foothold in my mind: "If this doesn't go as planned, can they take away my birthday?"

You see, I love my birthday. It's a moment of reflection and appreciation for me. I love the sincere messages and hearing from old friends. My birthday fills me with gratitude.

The question "If this doesn't go as planned, can they take away my birthday?" is incredibly silly but so are most of the things we fear. They're mostly in our heads. There is no bear, no dragon, and no actual physical threat.

It's fear of ridicule, of judgement, of failure.

And deep down it's subconsciously tied to a fear of being kicked out of "your crew." This could be your family, friends at school, or peers at work.

As I stood there in the Louvre, hesitating, 10 seconds turned into 30. Thirty seconds turned into a minute. People were milling about all around me, and my inner doubter was winning. I couldn't do it. I walked past a confused-looking Melissa and out of the gallery. She came out to find me pacing and mumbling to myself.

I was remembering Seoul and how my hesitation won that time. It stung. There was no way I could let that happen again. I asked myself "Could they take away my birthday?" Obviously that was a stupid question. It made me smile for a moment. OK, so what was the absolute worst thing that could happen, I asked myself. An angry security guard might yell at us in French as they escorted us out of the building. It would feel like a scene in a movie. We'd then have an epic tale to tell about getting kicked out of the most famous museum in the world for dancing.

I looked at Melissa. "I'm ready," I said.

"I know you can do this" was her response.

I went back to my spot, took a deep breath, and pressed play. I felt the music flow through my body and let it guide my movements. There was no stopping me once I started. I danced with my eyes closed. I danced as if I were alone in the room. Other than getting the stink eye from one security guard, nothing happened. We didn't get kicked out and no one took away my birthday.

I'd go on to dance in front of the Eiffel Tower, the Arc de Triomphe, and the Sacré-Coeur Basilica that week, but the Louvre was the hardest. It was the first.

It was indoors. I could get weird looks or be asked to stop at the other locations, but no one could kick me out of the outdoor places. They could have at the Louvre, but they didn't.

Once we got back home to Toronto I edited the dancing clips together into a short video. Two things struck me as I was doing the editing:

1. Rewatching the footage of me dancing on the steps in front of Sacré-Coeur Basilica, I noticed that there were dozens of people on the stairs in front of me, behind me, and walking two feet beside me. No one gave a shit. No one was looking. No one cared. What I realized was that we frequently hold ourselves back from expressing ourselves because we're worried about what others will think. The reality is that others aren't thinking about us nearly as much as we believe. They're too caught up in their own heads.
2. What was the cost of inaction in other parts of my life? How else was I letting fear guide my decisions?

The video seems so surreal that some assumed it was shot on a green screen. It's awesome to hear people's reaction when they realize that it really is me dancing in front of the Eiffel Tower, the Arc de Triomphe, and in the Louvre. Sharing the video online allowed me to bring together things that I love: music, dancing, and inspiring others to push past their fears.

Getting down in front of the Arc de Triomphe

40

Five Years From Now

I'd been bouncing between running my own businesses and working for others for a couple of decades. I'd had good runs with different businesses, but never enough to sustain my entrepreneur ambitions in the long term.

By 2018 I found myself in a leadership role in a small tech company that actually had a greater purpose. It was using technology to help the world by tracking and predicting the spread of infectious disease. I had a good salary, I was in a supportive relationship, and I was lucky enough to be able to go on fun vacations a couple of times a year with a partner that I loved. By most external metrics, I had made it.

The tech industry in Toronto was booming and I was being invited to speak on panels and sit on advisory boards. My job wasn't simply how I was paying the bills, I was also becoming a member of a community.

The tech and startup scene is full of entrepreneurial rebels: Unconventional thinkers looking to disrupt how things are done in all areas of business, including creating environments where employees feel genuinely supported as whole humans—something that was important to me. When you combine all this with the messages I was getting from recruiters offering me new roles on an almost weekly basis, my future seemed bright if I stayed on this path.

The problem was that whenever I took time to slow things down and reflect, I was filled with an overwhelming feeling that I wasn't living up to my potential. That I was meant to do more.

But now I was older and had two kids and a mortgage. I struggled to imagine how I could possibly break free. My dreams to do something with deeper meaning were fading under the pressure of the golden handcuffs.

I was following the easy path being set out in

front of me. Letting fear hold me back from taking action. While I was busy being afraid to listen to my heart, I convinced myself that maybe taking a new job, with a fancier title and salary increase, would fix this gnawing feeling of something missing. So I started entertaining the messages from recruiters and began interviewing.

It was a throwaway question at the end of a 90-minute interview for another job that snapped me out of it.

"Where do you see yourself in five years?" asked one of the startup co-founders sitting across from me.

The answer that came out of my mouth surprised me just as much as them.

"A coach," I said. The words just fell out. It's an idea I'd had before, but my self-defeating thoughts had never previously let me state it publicly.

Who the heck was I to say I could be a coach? What qualifications did I have? The world didn't need another fucking self-help person! Plus, how could I ever earn a living and take care of my family as a coach?

But there it was, now out in the open, and there was no putting it back in its cage once it was free.

The more I reflected on it, the more it was glaringly obvious that I had to find a way to follow through. After all, it was the leadership development and coaching parts of my job that put the pep in my step at the office. I found it incredibly rewarding to see a seasoned leader have an "aha" about small changes they could make that would have drastic impacts. I love helping people see their potential and then nudging them towards it.

Now I had to figure out how. I had been bold and brave enough to declare I wanted something and make it happen in the past. It was time to do it again.

41

Habit Tracking

"How do you achieve with consistency?"

It's a question that I had asked myself plenty of times before. I'd be "smashing it" in certain areas of life or business, while completely drowning in others. It's what happens when you focus on the big sexy goals without building the regular routines needed to bring the attractive final outcomes to life, piece by piece.

Like you, I had heard many times how important habits were to success. I had read other books about habits, but something about James Clear's book *Atomic Habits* hit differently. Its memorable stories made it easy to read and sold me on the compounding impact of focusing on habits, while it's practical framework made it seem simple and doable.

I'd had a morning routine on and off in the past but it came and went depending on what I was doing in my life. I knew I felt better on the days when I did my boot-up morning sequence but I struggled to stick with it.

Based on what I learned in the book, I started an experiment that included:

- Stacking habits, where I paired habits together so that one naturally flowed into the other (cold shower → stretches and exercises → meditation → journalling).
- Making my habits obvious, by installing a pull-up bar in a highly visible place and leaving my journal out so it would also act as a visual cue.
- Making embracing habits attractive by following habits-focused people online. It was the equivalent of me joining a virtual culture where my desired behaviour was the norm.
- Making it easy by focusing on the mini-habits that were the "on-ramps" to the bigger habits I desired. For example, I would say that

I'd just start with a cold shower and could change it afterwards if I wanted (I rarely did), or I'd commit to doing only three pull-ups (once I started, I rarely stopped).

- Making it satisfying by using a habit tracker where I got the satisfaction of checking the boxes and seeing my streak grow.
- Making a commitment to myself that I wouldn't miss two days in a row. Unexpected things could happen and throw off one day, but I couldn't miss two days in a row.
- Making my habits attractive by creating external accountability.

I decided to share my experiment and my journey publicly on Instagram. It's what created the external accountability for me. I hoped that it might encourage others, too.

The results of adopting a "habits first" approach surprised me. I felt a massive boost to my energy, my mental health, and my physical strength. My confidence increased and so did my ability to focus. It allowed me to create the consistency that had previously eluded me. All of this from committing to a morning sequence that included all of four things.

Meeting my habits idol, James Clear

42
Pop Fly

Once I started peeling back the layers of bullshit I was saying to myself, I couldn't stop. I kept asking what "truths" did I believe about myself that might actually not be true?

It led me to realize that I had been holding on to one terrible belief since I was seven. I was a scrawny kid who didn't feel particularly strong, and an incident during the short time that I played baseball in grade school cemented this negative conviction about myself for decades: "I'm physically weak and not good at sports."

I was in centre field when a pop fly came my way. The ball went high up, giving me lots of time to put myself in position under it. I fumbled the catch and got the ball in the face.

My team was upset and I ended up with a big black eye. I was teased for weeks and had a shining reminder of how weak I was anytime I looked in the mirror.

When reviewing my behaviour and decisions that followed in life, they played into this belief. I avoided sports as much as possible and never pushed myself physically. As I grew taller, I struggled with coordination and used it to reinforce this "truth." I carried the belief that I was weak well into my adult life.

When I did pursue physical activities that I enjoyed such as dancing and skateboarding, I still held back and avoided anything that required real physical strength.

I almost couldn't believe it once I started connecting all the dots. A decision I made as a seven-year-old kid had shaped so much of my life.

I now hold a new belief that I'm strong and physically fit. I know that I have the power to increase my strength by pushing myself. I've been doing push-ups, crunches, and pull-ups daily for over two years. I've added muscle mass and have never felt better physically.

The wildest part of making this shift is that I had someone call me athletic for the first time in my entire life within two months of changing my belief about my physical abilities and starting my new exercise routine. I changed my internal belief about myself, started acting in accordance with it, and it was now being reflected back to me by others.

43

Halfway There

Birthdays are reflective times for me. They make me pause and re-evaluate my life. Am I happy with where I'm at? Do I feel good about the trajectory? Am I using my gifts and contributing?

The annual check-in allows me to amplify my feelings of gratitude when things are going well and do the reflection needed to make changes when things feel off.

For my 40th birthday, I wanted to do something special. It was a milestone and I knew that meant people would give me extra airtime because of it. I was in an incredible place mentally and feeling excited about life. The goal was to use the extra attention I would get to pay it forward.

I felt pulled to do something memorable and impactful. I wanted to design a unique event where people could learn, grow, and have fun. I got the idea for an interactive workshop. I'd thrown music events and parties before, but never something like this. I spent weeks planning, organizing, and creating material for the event. It became a part-time job.

Here's the info that went on the invite:

"Life moves pretty fast. If you don't stop and look around once in a while, you could miss it."

\- Ferris Bueller

What if I brought together some of the smartest, most caring, empathetic, creative, driven, and curious people I know for a one-of-a-kind event? This is the question I asked myself when contemplating my upcoming milestone birthday.

I'm turning the big 4-0! Or, as my kids have so elegantly put it by singing me Bon Jovi lyrics, I'm statistically "halfway there." In the past, these landmark birthdays have led to deep reflection: Where am I at in life? Am I happy? Am I contributing? Am I doing what I'm meant to be doing? I'm glad to report that I'm feeling pretty darn fantastic about the current responses to these types of questions.

I'm halfway there and I'm overflowing with gratitude. I'm inviting you and a guest to join me and some of my favourite humans to take a moment to pause and celebrate. We'll pause to reflect, to laugh, to appreciate, and maybe even learn something new. Then we'll celebrate and shake our tail feathers to acknowledge this wild and wonderful life.

WHAT'S GOING DOWN?

- Fun activities & games
- Kickass conversations
- Silliness & laughs
- Learning
- A hypnotist show

HOW THE EVENT WORKS:

PART 1 :: WE PAUSE :: 8 p.m. -10 p.m. > We'll mingle, play games, learn, laugh, and be dazzled by the power of the subconscious mind with a hypnotist show.

PART 2 :: WE CELEBRATE :: 10 p.m. onwards > The lights will get dim and we'll celebrate with a dance party.

WHAT TO WEAR?

'80s rock themed costumes are highly encouraged. Yes, that means torn jeans, tight leather pants, mesh shirts, big hair....all that!

Why? Because life is more enjoyable if you get out of your routines and let yourself be silly from time to time.

WHAT YOU'LL GET:

FUN: The theme, the games, the hypnotist show—it's all set up in a way to help you have a whale of a time.

INSPIRATION & INSIGHTS: You'll be exposed to new ideas and activities that bring them to life.

COMMUNITY: You'll be sharing experiences with a room full of smart, empathic, driven, creative, curious, and self-realized dope-ass humans.

COST:

The event is free. All that we ask is that you bring your energy, your participation, and an open mind.

On the night of the event, Melissa helped me decorate the venue with posters containing funny and inspiring messages, plants, hundreds of mini disco balls, and an insane amount of balloons.

The mix of people who came couldn't have been more eclectic: Childhood friends, old rave buddies, previous co-workers, DJs, and new friends I had met at the leadership seminar.

There were four stations that people went through as part of the workshop:

1. When you walked in the door you were invited to pause, close your eyes, let your thoughts from the day go, focus on your breath, and pay attention to the sounds of the room you were now standing in. It was a grounding exercise. A meditation. But I intentionally didn't call it either of those.

2. The next station had cut-out hearts with the prompt: "I'm so happy and grateful for….." written on them. People filled in the blank with things they were happy and grateful for. We stuck all the completed hearts to the wall. The wall of hearts then made for a cool mural for people to take pictures in front of.

3. The third station is where things got a bit silly by combining a communication exercise with drawing. Two people sat back to back. One looked at an image and instructed the other person on what to draw without telling them what they were drawing.

   If it was a picture of a cat's head, you couldn't say, "It's a cat." You had to say "draw a big circle and then two semi-circles on top of it." It showed people how much we assume and how much communication we take for granted. The drawings that came out of the exercise were hilarious and plenty of laughs ensued.

4. The fourth exercise is where things got serious. It was a deep active listening exercise where people had to practise full body listening. It means your feet are flat on the ground, your body is squared up to the other person, and you are using your entire body to listen, without interruption—no waiting for your turn to talk. The person talking had to talk for four minutes straight about the answer to this question:

   Is there something that you've dreamed of doing for a long time? Why haven't you done it?

   There was a bonus second question if you wanted to dive deeper with a second round:

   Tell me how you want to love and be loved?

With this kind of exercise, things get profound and intimate. I saw one couple hugging with tears in their eyes after the exercise. Another one thanked me and said it was the deepest conversation they had in years.

The workshop ended with my friend Gilles, a hypnotist, talking about the power of our subconscious beliefs. He then brought up volunteers to demonstrate how influential the subconscious mind is. He had some people on stage feeling absolutely stuck to their chairs simply because he told them that they were, and others were answering to completely different names than their own thanks to his hypnotic suggestions. He mixed teaching with comedy and it was hilarious.

When the activities were over, the lights went down and some friends and I DJed. Not everyone "got" what I was trying to do, and that's fine. But I saw that it sparked things in those who went in with an open mind. People thanked me, told me they had a blast, that they had learned things, and that they'd never been to that kind of event before.

I had achieved my goal of using my birthday as a platform to create an impactful and memorable event. This was what I was meant to do and I needed to figure out how to get more of it in my life.

Melissa and I in front of the wall of grateful hearts at my Halfway There birthday party

44

You Don't Need Us

As I was building the confidence to leave my job and focus on coaching, I signed up for a weekend course at the Fairmont Royal York hotel in Toronto. The program promised to teach me coaching and business development skills to "naturally ensure my long-term success in this rewarding, expanding profession."

I intentionally chose this particular session as the founder of the organization, Derrick Sweet, was going to be leading the training. He had been coaching people for over 20 years and his company had trained over 12,000 coaches. He had left a successful career in the financial industry to go into coaching and was the author of several books. He seemed like someone

I could definitely learn from.

Derrick greeted the group as we arrived. He stood over six feet tall, had a gray goatee, and was wearing a brightly coloured Hawaiian shirt. Wanting to get as much from the weekend as possible, I sat near the front.

Derrick wasted no time showing us that he was quirky, spoke with passion, and had a contagious laugh that almost didn't seem real. He was clearly someone who chose to be happy and was unapologetically himself. It was refreshing. Trying to imagine him as an investment firm vice-president in a suit was hard. He had intentionally and completely reinvented his life.

We spent two days learning frameworks for leading coaching sessions, tools to use with clients, the basics of Neuro-Linguistic Programming (commonly called NLP), and some high level business advice, including ways to think about choosing your niche.

I was soaking it all up. Submerged in a learning environment full of creative and empathic people, I felt completely in my element. Derrick was a spirited speaker who knew how to intentionally change the pacing and emphasis of what he was saying to fully captivate his audience.

Not only was I loving what I was learning, but

I could also see myself possibly even delivering the material. Maybe this could be a way to leverage my training experience as I shifted into coaching? Derrick already had a successful company and the curriculum to go with it. It could be a safe way for me to start, I thought. I figured that they ran these sessions in multiple cities—would it be crazy to ask Derrick about the possibility of becoming a facilitator?

As things were wrapping up on Sunday evening, I felt even more assured that I was on the right path and I hadn't even gotten my biggest takeaway from the weekend yet. I wanted to personally thank Derrick for everything but several of my classmates were huddled around him, taking pictures, and asking questions.

I waited a few minutes but people had a lot to say and there was a lineup of others already waiting to speak with him. I grew impatient and walked away. As I got to the end of the hall near the top of the stairs that led down to the hotel lobby, my inner voice said to go back. I pivoted mid-step and turned around.

I waited patiently for the last person to finish.

"Thanks for such an incredible weekend, Derrick. I learned so much and you're exceptional at what you do," I said.

"Thank you, I really appreciate that," he replied.

"What would be the steps if I wanted to work with you and lead these seminars?" I then asked. The words came out of my mouth before I had a chance to stop them.

"You'd have to find a city with a demand where there's not someone already doing them," he said.

He then paused and looked me intently in the eyes before carrying on.

"I'd love to have you with us, but you don't need us. You're going to have incredible success on your own."

I was taken aback. He continued.

"You're meant to do this. This work is clearly from the heart for you. You have a magnetic quality about you and people trust you. You don't need us."

I was speechless.

He was calling me out for thinking small and pointing out potential in me that I didn't even see in myself. That's the power of coaching. **You can't read the label from inside the jar.**

45

December 10th

"Quit my job by December 10th."

I wrote the words on a post-it note and stuck it to the wall in our kitchen. I didn't know how, but I knew by writing it down and giving it a deadline that it would become real. I'd make it happen.

It was an arbitrary date, December 10th is my birthday and it was far enough out that I was able to create some belief that I could actually do it.

In the following months, I took courses, devoured books, hired mentors, and joined programs. I did everything possible to acquire the knowledge and skills needed to make the successful leap, all while fuelling a belief in myself that it was happening.

Even though I only had a few clients at the time, in November I told my boss that I planned to leave. If I was going to make this work, I had to go all in and make it a must. I let them know that I was leaving in January. I was in a senior role and on the leadership team. The two months would give them plenty of time to backfill my position while hopefully giving me a chance to build up my business before no longer having a salary.

I wasn't going to meet my target date of being out by December 10th, but January wasn't bad. I felt pretty good about it.

I posted a video on LinkedIn announcing that I was quitting my job to focus on coaching people full time. I outright owned this major shift I was making. If I was doing this, I wasn't going to be meek about it. I was also very intentional about declaring the kind of people I knew I was meant to serve.

I had successfully leveraged social media and unconventional marketing approaches with my past businesses. I knew that if I tried to speak to everyone with my content, that it would actually resonate with no one. When declaring who I was meant to coach with my new venture, I was conscious in saying that

I was serving self-aware, driven, curious, creative people who have a love for life, and have already committed time, energy, and money working on themselves. They are people who simply need my help getting over the finish line.

The response was almost instant.

The video went viral and got over 20,000 views, hundreds of likes, and loads of comments. Suddenly, I was flooded with inquiries from people who wanted to work with me. It was wild.

Within days I was getting up at 6 a.m. to work on my coaching business before going into the office, and scheduling calls with clients over lunch to try and keep up. The choice I now faced: Turn down clients as I was launching my new business, or burn out.

I went back to my boss.

"I know I said I was leaving in January. I'm sorry, but I actually have to go in two weeks," I told her.

My last day ended up being December 6th, four days before my initial goal.

The sticky note that was on our kitchen wall for half a year

46

Take a Chance on Me

As 2020 was coming to an end, I put on a free online workshop to help people process the wild year that we had all had.

The holiday season tends to stir reflection, goal setting, and new intentions. People are thinking about how they want next year to be different and hopefully better. I wanted to help people get the most out of 2020 and figure out what they wanted to intentionally take from this once in a lifetime pandemic experience.

I ran the workshop twice and at different times of day to allow people from various continents to attend. The attendees were a mix of strangers, people I was acquainted with online, and some of my coaching clients.

One of the questions I asked participants to reflect on and answer was: What's the nicest thing someone did for you this year?

The following day, I got this beautiful message from my client, Karen:

"In response to 'What's the nicest thing someone did for you this year.' It's YOU. You took me on as a client. You took a chance on me. And you continue to help me in a way that no one ever has in my life! I am so grateful for you."

I was sitting in my car after running some errands when I got her note. My physical response was instant: Tears ran down my face. I was crying glorious tears of gratitude.

Since launching Growth Habit I've helped over 200 people and worked with clients in 13 different countries.

I've helped people launch and grow their businesses and their impact, including:

- A 24-year-old entrepreneur who has founded a growing ed-tech startup that's received over half a million dollars in funding to prepare people for the future of work

- A coach who quit their toxic corporate job and launched a social impact business that's on track to donate $37,000 to a charity for grieving children in their first year
- A young entrepreneur who's on pace to hit a million dollars in revenue in 2021 and who's using their success to hire friends and family members so they can all succeed together

I'm no longer selling drugs. I'm selling people on believing in themselves, betting on their dreams, taking bold action, and creating a life and business on their terms that has both meaning and purpose.

47

Loose Goals

I never intended on coaching coaches.

I knew I wanted to take things I'd learned in my life to help others feel more empowered, joyful, creative, aligned, and purposeful. That was the big goal.

If you would have asked me while I was still doing coaching on the side, I would have told you that I was a creativity coach. I had a creative background, I loved artists, and I knew different ways to help people be more consistently creative. Some of my first clients included a recording artist, a photographer, a music producer, and a writer.

But then people started showing up and asking me if I could help them with their habits. They'd seen what I had shared on Instagram about the implementation of my morning routine and the impact habits were having on my life. People messaged and said "I want you to help me do THAT. Get better at habits."

I paused and reflected on it. I knew how to help people with their habits. I would enjoy doing it. It had helped me tremendously, and I knew it would help me help other people become better versions of themselves. It wasn't a tough decision. So when I quit my job and launched Growth Habit, I told the world that I was a "Habit Strategist."

I did that for a while and then I realized at some point that 11 of my first 12 clients were entrepreneurs. I asked myself why that was. I'd been an entrepreneur on and off my entire life. I loved that entrepreneurs are action-driven, aren't afraid of failure, are willing to get messy and roll up their sleeves, are looking to solve interesting problems, and are carving their own path. I identify with all that. They're my people.

So I started saying that I was an "entrepreneur coach that helped people achieve more consistent results by creating empowering habits that last."

Then people came asking me if I coached coaches. They wanted to know how I got inbound inquiries and clients overseas. I said no to the first two people. I thought "I've got no business coaching coaches." But when the third coach asked to "pick my brain" in a 10-day span, I thought, Huh, this might be the universe trying to tell me something again.

The point is, you need to hold your big goals loosely, create commitment to moving forward, take the first step, and adjust along the way. If I had waited for everything to be perfect, I wouldn't have started.

Now I'm loving the work that I do, using my creativity while knowing with certainty that I'm making an impact on others, that I have control of my schedule, and that I'm making more money than ever before. Given my new belief around money, that means I'm providing a lot of value.

It's the same approach I took with creating this book. I'd had the desire to write a book for years but had no idea what it would look like. I knew the bigger goal was similar to my coaching: Write something that would help others feel more empowered, joyful, creative, aligned, and purposeful. At one point, I thought I was going to just take content from one of my courses and repurpose it into a book, but that didn't feel right.

When I realized that it could be a collection of stories from my journey because the tales from my adventures seemed to resonate so deeply with others, the question became "How?" It began with me making a decision that I was absolutely doing it. Then I started taking action without knowing exactly how I'd pull it off.

I then:

- Hired a book coach to guide me on my journey and help me get quicker results
- Set a deadline for when the first draft would be done
- Created a daily writing habit

As I started writing more, the larger story arc of what initially felt like disjointed stories from my life began coming together. I was able to more clearly define that I wanted the book to be loved by creative, curious, entrepreneurial, rebellious, and empathic people who desire to live a fuller life.

I wanted *you* as the reader to feel that you have permission to lead a creative and unorthodox life on your terms, that fills you with purpose and meaning. The book evolved along the way until it became what you are now holding in your hands.

So what are you holding back on? What burning inner desire are you pretending isn't there?

48

Die Before They Do

Once I had submitted the first draft of the book to my book coach and editor, Cat, Melissa and I went out on a date to celebrate. It was a bit of an odd day as I had been crying a bunch. I'd found out that a friend had passed away the day before. Another one gone too soon.

It was a warm evening and we were on an outdoor patio of a busy downtown Toronto street. I was sharing some reflections as we enjoyed Mediterranean food.

"Writing the book has made me realize how many social groups I've been a part of and how many incredible people I've been lucky to learn from," I shared.

I started listing them off:

"All the army kids I grew up with, especially the ones in Borden. The Barrie raver crew, the Banting crowd, all the places I've worked, the people I met through music in Toronto, the friends I've made in all the cities I've played, people from around the world that I connected with through the music industry, the supportive people in the Toronto tech industry, and now a whole new community in the realm of coaching. And I'm just skimming and summarizing here," I said.

My eyes were welling up now.

"Some aren't lucky enough to have that many people to learn from, to laugh with, and share memories with. I'm so grateful. The downside that hit me earlier today is that I'm going to have five times as many friends die."

My breath caught in my throat. I was struggling to get the words out.

"What if it isn't like that?" Melissa asked.

I was confused by her statement, but before I could even ask what she meant, she continued.

"What if you die before they do?"

She bit her tongue before saying anything else to see how I'd react.

I started laughing, loudly. Melissa joined in. The others dining near us didn't appreciate how loud we were being.

It was dark but it was also funny and possibly true. There's no guarantee that I'll wake up tomorrow and who knows what's in store for you.

Don't wait.

Don't wait for the eulogy. Or to say I love you. Or to start listening to the voice inside you that's saying you're meant for more. The world needs your creativity, your ideas, your art, and your message. The cost might be letting go of some things you are deeply attached to, including perhaps who you believed yourself to be, or what others expected of you. Venturing into the unknown can be scary, but regret over what could have been is the heavier price to pay.

As Wayne Dyer said, "Don't die with your music still in you."

P.S. Jim Carrey, if you're reading this, let's do lunch.

Acknowledgements

There are so many people to thank for helping me reach this moment. Melissa, thank you for believing in me even when I doubted myself. You've shown me a new level of relationship as a loving care buddy and parent to the kids. This book simply would not exist without your love and support. I want to thank my kids for giving me purpose, laughter, and lessons to learn. Monika, thank you for being the best co-parent imaginable, truly. Mom, I'm so grateful to you for instilling so much empathy in me. Pops, thank you for supporting me in my crazy ventures, even when you didn't understand them. Anthony, I love you. Catalina, you helped me take this pile of seemingly random stories and mould them into a cohesive and sensible whole. This book is 1000 times better because of you. Moriah, thank you for all your support in keeping me organized and helping me bring this book to life.

There are so many others I'm grateful for: Adele Desloges, Adrian Morris, Alec Melkonian, Alex D, Alex Goldau, Ali Cheung, Alicia Andrews, Alison Gareh, Allison Sophia, Andy Akiva Johnson, Ann Meiring, Andre Sousa, Ari Barmapov, Brian Bobroff, Brittany "Britz Bitts" Card, Brittany Cornish, Bryan Farbs, Byron Van Pelt, Candace Forsyth, Cassandra Hui, Cassidy Thedorf, Chelsea Verrette, Chris Atwell, Chris Kotsy for capturing so many incredible pictures, Christine Veda, Claire "Sausage" Parsons, Colin Big League Chu, Colin Mobey, Connie Icon, Corey Rideout, Craig Pettigrew, Chris Dustin, Cy Charney, Cyrus Songad, Dan Melon, Dan Monic, Daneal Charney, Darla-Jean Patterson, Dave Saddler, David Mclean, David T, Derrick Sweet, Diliana Popova, DJ Dan, DJ Icey, Don Red Lion, Doug Lawson, Dre Luca, Drew Smart, Dylan ill.Gates, Duane Dawson, Eireann Keating, Elliot Smith, Erica Kelly, Eroca Vermett, Evan G, everyone @ BlueDot, everyone @ Shambhala, Fabienne Raphael, Francisco Mahfuzz, George Hatiras, Giles Bernard, Ginette Black, Glen Webster, Glenn Zujew, Geoff Curtis, Grant Chi, Greg Witz, Gurpreet K. Man, Heather McHughan, Heidi Forman, Irish Seno, Jacqueline Yeung, Jafar Owainati, James Eaton, James Mr Brown, Jamie Tobin, Jason Wisdom, Jay +

Trevor Lambert, Jay Cleary, Jas Der, Jeff "Jefr" Taylor and all in the incredible Root Society family, Jen Jones, Jennifer Brick, Jer Fink, Jerome Robins, Jesse Fritz, Jessica Palombella, Ji In Kim, Jo Rothchild, Joe Lyons-Rising, Joel + Steph @ Coda, Joel Mau5, John Dion, Jon Belliveau, Jonny Belinko, Josh Jelo, Joshua Cruz, June Caloroso, Justin Pintala, Justin Tyce, Kamran Khan, Karen Choi, Kate "Kate" Johnson, Katie Carpenter, Katy Chan, Keirsten Caird, Keith Mackenzie, Kenny Kendall, Kevin Bracken, Kevin Logan Jr., Kevin "Red Turtle" Yu, Kim Mussa, Kim Okabe, Kris Chau, Kristin Michelle, Lauree Akhtar, Lauren Smith, Lekan Olawoye, Leo Perri, Liquid Todd, Logan Hudak, Lori Ferrara, Lori McIntosh, Lucia Lewis, Lynn Lapierre, Manny Paranoid Jack, Manousos + Jenn @ Footwerk, Marcia Chiclet, Marcus Chan, Maria Buscemi, Martin Krafty Kuts, Matt Mealing, Matt Traynor, Matt Waite, Melissa Godbout, Melissa James, Michael Deko-ze, Michael Lossier, Michael "Andy Poolhall" Sweenie-Lane, Michael Warchol, Mike Atrix, Missy Marie, Miz Megs, Monica Broekhoven-Bellini, Monte Clark, Nadia + Wallis Wallis, Nat Flipside, Natasha Kaan, Nick Kopa for the incredible book design, Nick Raeburn, Nicole Ferreira, Nizar Hasan, Noriko Yokoi, Nunich, Pablo Spinz, Pat Brown + Jude Brown (pretty confident I'd be dead without you two), Patricia + Daniel Leung, Patrick Harpin + the Montréal Frogland Breakers crew, Patrick Robles + France Mateo @ Breakfest, Paul Walker, Peter Manzone, PJ Stephen, Prieeyya Kaur Kesh, Rain + Zach @ SEEDS, Reid Speed, Rich "Lazy" Billis, Richard Poplak, Rich-e-Rich, Robb Meir, Robbie Picard, Roy Itzhaki, Saira Gangji, Sarah Mackinnon Dowell, Shane Wiley, Shannon Dee, Shannon Shields, Sheldon Street, Sherene Elizabeth, Shianne Zaba, Simon Paul, Sky Barbarick, Spencer Brown, Stepanie Fleming, Steve Duda, Stu Bass Kleph, Sue Easby, Susan and Gunter Meyer, Sydney Bertram, Tab Daigle,Tamir Moscovici, Tarah Walsh, Taylor "TK" Gresnor, Ted Killin, Teresa Holmes, Terry Hooligan, Terry Mullan, the awesome LinkedIn community, the Banting crew, the Barrie raver crew, the Borden crew, the Eastern Bloc crew, the entire Dose + Lifeforce crew, the Jackass crew, the Toronto Breakbeat crew, Thomas "Outlaw" Milan, TJR, the Victoria Hush crew, Toby Emerson, Todd Holland, Todd Wautier, Tom Dunn, Tomb, Tracy Ticky Ty, Travis Lachner, Trevor Spilt Milk, Vanessa Recine, Wayne Mealing, Wes Henderson, Will Low Steppa, Willar De Naranja, Zak Hemraj.

And those who left us too soon:

Darrel Nimigeon, Don Berns, Galen Macdonald, Gary Scott, Jay Hamilton, Jessie Daniel, John Horvath, Jonny "funkNstyle" Williams, Marky Kavalir, Mike "vs Zero" Grefner, Pietro "Redeyez" Long, Tim Taro.

Head over to:

Growthhabit.org

You'll find free training on:

- How to find an aligned and profitable niche that you're excited to serve
- How to create content that attracts Dream Clients
- How to grow on Linkedin

About the Author

Robb Gilbear is an entrepreneur coach and mentor. He founded Growth Habit in 2019 and has helped more than 200 people from countries around the world launch and grow their businesses. He is passionate about helping people create new realities for themselves, and works with clients to help them define their unique message so they can deeply connect with those they're meant to serve. Robb lives in Toronto with his partner, Melissa, and two kids, and although he officially retired as a DJ, he still plays the odd show.

If you enjoyed this book and the stories within, could you take a moment to write a review on the site where you purchased it? It's the best way to ensure that others find out about the book and it would mean a lot to me.

Thanks so much,

-Robb

Manufactured by Amazon.ca
Bolton, ON

40758729R00152